THE GREATEST DISASTERS

OF THE 20th CENTURY

This edition published in 1989 by
Tiger Books International Ltd,
3 Friars Lane, Richmond, Surrey TW9 1NL

© Marshall Cavendish Limited 1975, 1989

ISBN 1-870461-65-7

Printed in Portugal

•R.M.S. TITANIC•

THE GREATEST DISASTERS
OF THE 20th CENTURY

TIGER BOOKS INTERNATIONAL
LONDON

Contents

All of the above were written by
Frances Kennett, with the exception
of the last six chapters (marked ★),
which were written by Jean Trier.

*8/9 Ermenonville Forest after the crash of the
DC10*

9

Introduction

Disaster is unlike anything else in human experience. It strikes quickly, it changes the lives of all it touches, and its effects are felt long after the event. And, perhaps more important, its forces are largely outside the control of the people whom it most affects.

Disasters are frequently the result of natural phenomena, themselves unaffected by the actions of mere human beings. But modern technology is capable of predicting hurricanes, tornadoes and even earthquakes. As often as not the warnings issued before such an event are ignored to a notorious degree. The real disaster, in terms of human life, almost always comes from this uniquely human failure to heed the signals. Before Mont Pelèe erupted on the island of Martinique in 1902, there had been plenty of warning signals – but the authorities and the press actively disregarded them and encouraged people to stay, resulting in the entire population of St Pierre, 30,000 people, being killed.

Other disasters are built on human error, and are usually compounded by it. The 'unsinkable' *Titanic* sank because one person after another failed to heed the danger presented by a deadly pack of icebergs in the North Atlantic; the general reluctance even to believe that such a tragedy was possible meant that there were not enough lifeboats available and most of the ones that were provided were lowered with only a few people in each. 1503 people died on that cold night. More recently, 346 people died when a Turkish Airlines DC10 crashed outside Paris after a series of human ineptitudes resulted in the failure of an airport attendant to close a baggage door properly. And, of course, there was the tragedy of the *Herald of Free Enterprise* in 1987, also arising from human failing.

The disasters discussed here have all made an impact on our world. Either they are the worst events of their kind in our century or they have had a profound effect on our 'folk' culture, like Aberfan and the explosion of the space shuttle Challenger. Or they have caused the authorities responsible to think again about safety procedures which would hopefully prevent a recurrence of disaster, such as the explosion at a nylon manufacturing plant in Flixborough, and the terrible fire in King's Cross underground station.

They do not include disasters that result from acts of war: hence we have included the *Titanic* but not the *Lusitania*, the explosion at Chernobyl but not Hiroshima. Disastrous as these are, they are created by acts of aggression rather than by natural events or human neglect.

May 8, 1902
Eruption of Mont Pelèe

Below *The town of St Pierre, Martinique, nestles at the foothills of the volcanic peak of Mont Pelèe.*

Right *Desolation was all that remained of St Pierre after the cloud of ash and steam.*

At the turn of the century, Martinique was a pretty, prosperous French colony, nestling among the Lesser Antilles in the Caribbean. A favoured spot for summer visitors from France, the island luxuriated in tropical flowers, banana trees, sugar cane plantations and dense forests.

Its natural profusion came from the soil: rich dark volcanic matter spewed forth over centuries by the island's biggest mountain, the volcanic peak of Mont Pelèe. 4583 feet high, Pelèe dominated the landscape at the northern end of the island. Just below lay the main town of St Pierre, with 30,000 inhabitants. Further south and on the same west side of the island stood the principal port, Fort de France.

The peaceful colonial existence of the island's natives and French settlers was strangely disturbed in the early months of 1902. Although Mont Pelèe was known to be an active volcano, it had never done more than cause a few rumbles or spit out a little ash. Its main crater held a beautiful mirror-like lake, which was a favourite picnic spot for visitors from France.

Suddenly in early April, steam and great hissing noises poured from the crater. Volcanic ash began to rain down on the Indian settlements nestling in the forests of Mont Pelèe's foothills. By April 25, the activity had become so fierce and continuous that the French authorities sent a scientific commission up the mountain to investi-

gate. A secondary crater, a little lower down than the main lake, was rapidly filling with water. Previously, it had been a dry hollow called the *Etang Sec*, or 'dry pool'. A new cinder cone, a product of volcanic activity, was pushing its way up through the boiling water and rising steam.

The commission seems to have approached this phenomenon with great scientific interest, but with little apprehension for people's safety. The island's main newspaper, *Les Colonies*, published the scientific finding: there was no reason to be afraid. In various editorial comments, the paper mocked those citizens who were beginning to express fears.

Nothing short of folly could have induced people to ignore nature's warnings. Life on Martinique became more unendurable day by day. A hideous odour of sulphur filled the air towards the end of April. The wife of the American consul, Mrs Prentiss, recorded, 'The smell of it is so strong that horses on the street stop and snort, and some of them drop in their harness and die of suffocation. Many of the people are obliged to wear wet handkerchiefs to protect them from the strong fumes of sulphur'.

A continuous pall of grey ash hung over the north end of the island. Trees looked as if a light snowstorm had descended; the Jardin des Plantes, where rare tropical blooms were reared for dispatch to the famous hothouse garden in Paris, was smothered in a film of silver: palms, ravenalas, mangoes, rubber trees, cacti and hibiscus were all drained of colour. Soon, birds dropped out of the sky, asphyxiated by ash and sulphur. By May 3, many businessmen in St Pierre put up their shutters, as prudent individuals moved bag and baggage to the southern part of the island.

Yet *Les Colonies* maintained its air of quiet mockery at the despondency. It prattled about possible excursions to see the wonder of nature at work. A setback occurred on May 5 when a giant boil of mud spewed out of Pelèe's crater and down the Rivière Blanche. It completely smothered the Guerin factory lying directly in its path, killing 30 employees inside. Now citizens began to flee in greater number. Yet on May 7, *Les Colonies* ran an interview with a distinguished French professor, M. Landes, in which he declared with confidence that Mont Pelèe presented 'no more danger to the inhabitants of St Pierre than does Vesuvius to those of Naples'. By modern safety standards this was hardly a great recommendation. The Italian volcano Vesuvius is chiefly famous for the great eruption of AD 79 that wiped out the towns of Pompeii, Stabiae and Herculaneum. It has seldom remained silent in its long history. In the 50 years between 1850 and 1900 it had erupted five times. Still, many citizens chose to ignore the evidence. That same day, May 7, the newspaper reported on the mass exodus and added, 'We confess we cannot understand this panic. Where could one be better off than at St Pierre?' While 300 citizens a day left, the town's population grew with the intake of refugees from the villages on Pelèe's slopes. The

May 7 newspaper carried a small footnote, 'Our offices being closed tomorrow, the next issue will appear on Friday.'

There never was another issue. At 4am on Thursday, May 8, a giant thunderstorm broke over Fort de France, lighting up the whole west coast of Martinique. At 7.30am the skies cleared, and from the port a high column of black smoke could be seen billowing up from Mont Pelèe. The cloud glistened with millions of shiny particles described by one eye witness as a 'whole cloud surface fairly scintillating with dancing lights'. Rumblings, explosive noises and then loud detonations filled the air for at least an hour.

The inhabitants of Fort de France gathered on the quayside to watch the strange scene taking place 14 miles to the north. At 8.50, a gigantic wave receded from the shores of the port and then flooded back to the brink at a height increased by at least two feet. At 9.18 a staggering flash of lightning shaped like a lightbulb filament or balloon looped across the northeast sky. The black cloud grew bigger and bigger, mushrooming, billowing, shooting out sparks that could be seen miles away. Lightning flashes and thunder filled the air. Orange serpents, S-shaped streaks of electrical discharges, produced spectacular effects against the black rolling mass.

This violent activity continued into the afternoon, culminating in a terrific storm. An eye witness in Fort de France recorded the final outburst. 'The steam cloud, with a velocity of 20mph came overhead, grey and tongue-shaped. It spread across the vault, producing darkness, when it reached the zenith, pebbles fell about the size of a chestnut, cold, and these became a rattling hail diminishing to the size of peas. Then fine grey ash followed. . . .'

From a ship just outside St Pierre itself, the

Above *The cloud of ash and steam hailed down stones the size of chestnuts on the city; hot grey ash set fire to wooden structures. Billowing clouds of steam crawled through the streets, and soon the whole of St Pierre was engulfed in flame and rubble.*
Right *The tower of Pelèe, made of thick lava, pushed upwards through the growing dome.*
Below right *A view of the volcanic storm clouds that billowed out of Pelèe's summit during the volcanic eruption. Thunder, flashing sparks and trails of curved lightning filled the air for miles around.*

eruption of Pelèe looked as if the mountain had blown to pieces. A cloud of fire and mud rolled down over the town, over the sea, over the ships. A great tidal wave crashed the vessels on to the shore, where they lay listing and smouldering, their top decks on fire.

St Pierre was totally engulfed in that billowing black cloud. All 30,000-odd people within its limits, many attending Ascension Day church services, were smothered and burned to death. The extraordinary feature of Pelèe's eruption was that very little lava-flow caused damage. People were killed by a blistering mixture of 1500°F steam and noxious gases. Just one citizen lived to tell the tale—a 28-year-old native shoemaker called Leon Comprère-Leandre.

'I was seated on a doorstep of my house which was in the southeast part of the city . . . all of a sudden I felt a terrible wind blowing, the earth began to tremble, and the sky suddenly became dark.' Leon ran inside, where he was joined by several other people off the street seeking shelter. They all lay down, and one by one succumbed to the heat and lack of oxygen. Leon himself lay in agony on his bed, his throat and lungs bursting with pain, waiting to die. 'My sense returned to me in perhaps an hour, my legs bleeding and covered in burns, I ran to Fonds-Saint-Denis, six kilometres from St Pierre. I heard no human cries . . . the entire city was aflame.'

Meanwhile at Fort de France, a ship was being prepared to sail north round the point that separated it from St Pierre. No news had come from the town, and the port people were anxious. The Vicar General of Fort de France, M. Parel, boarded the vessel and set sail for St Pierre. He made a historic record of the terrible scene that awaited the sea-borne party.

All the ships in the harbour were burning fiercely. The whole town was a mass of fire. 'No living soul', wrote M. Parel, 'appears in this desert of desolation, encompassed by appalling silence.' Mount Pelèe in the background was covered with a thick film of white ash, rising like an alpine peak above the ruins below. A region of eight to nine square miles was completely destroyed, and all the vegetation was killed for miles around. Three towns, St Pierre, Basse Pointe and Prêcheur, were obliterated by the black steam. M. Parel concluded, '. . . the city [of St Pierre] was laid to smouldering ruins, coated with ash-paste, and looking as if it were built of adobe plaster. What had before been the vivid colouring of houses of the tropics was now ashen grey.'

Yet worse disaster followed. On May 20 an earthquake shook the island, flattening the little that remained among the cinders of St Pierre and causing further damage to Fort de France. The editor of the newspaper, *Les Colonies*, had died in the first eruption; otherwise, he no doubt would have had something to say about the mass exodus that now took place. Thousands fled to the nearby islands of St Lucia, Guadeloupe and Trinidad or went further afield to new lives in France and the USA. As Vicar General M. Parel put it, 'It is no

Right The structure of a volcano. Fissures in the earth's crust allow molten rock and gases to erupt and a cone of solidified lava builds up.

Below Like the inhabitants of Martinique, the people of Pompeii ignored warnings and were caught by the eruption of Mt Vesuvius in AD79. Many bodies have been found perfectly preserved in ash where they fell in streets and homes.

Bottom Vesuvius last erupted in 1944, spewing its lava into the Bay of Naples below.

longer the exodus of the north to the south, but of all Martinique to foreign lands . . . I can but follow the example of Father Mary and of his fellow priests of the northern parishes. I shall be the last to leave Martinique.'

Out of the upheaval of Mont Pelèe, a giant obelisk rose up above the ash-filled valley. 'Spines' of this sort are created by extra-thick lava that pushes up through the growing dome in a straight pile instead of falling down the slope in a runny mass. This 'Tower of Pelèe' was a spectacular example of the phenomenon. At its maximum it rose 2000 feet high. Its destruction occurred in gradual stages. Explosions round its base as early as July 1903 caused it to crack and collapse. All the time, the volcano continued to roar and rumble, filling the sky with glowing colour and sparkling particles.

Several features of the Pelèe volcanic eruption make it unique among natural disasters. It caused a greater disturbance in the earth's magnetic field than any previously recorded. Sound waves from the explosions reached as far as 1000 miles away. The electric illumination of the sky and the giant serpents of lightning were extraordinary manifestations of the volcano's disturbance. The shock waves and earth tremors recorded reached almost to Krakatoa proportions—the great volcano in the straits of Sunda between Sumatra and Java had erupted in 1883, causing a mighty flood that killed 40,000 people on the Javanese coast. It was the greatest explosion in world history, and when it had ended, Krakatoa had disappeared. The explosions of Krakatoa were heard 2200 miles away. Spectacular sunsets lit up the skies all over the world for a year afterwards. Mont Pelèe provided the same brilliant red skies, and afterglows were reported off Venezuela, the coast of California, in Honolulu and in Europe from Italy to England. The steam and ash from Pelèe hurled up four to six miles into the sky. Krakatoa had spewed forth volcanic matter to a height of 50 miles.

That French expert, M. Landes, had mentioned Vesuvius as a reassuring comparison. What a strange prophecy. Just as the citizens of Pompeii were buried where they stood in a massive lava flow, so too St Pierre was wiped out in a matter of seconds. The curious difference was the absence of lava. Destruction was caused by superheated steam travelling at a speed of one and a half to three miles per minute as it left the summit.

The tragedy of Pelèe is the almost total absence of preparation by the citizens of St Pierre. Ignoring all signs, they lived from day to day in a state of suspended judgement. It is perhaps the strangest and most dangerous of human reactions to impending disaster, and one that is extremely difficult to overcome.

April 14, 1912
Sinking of the Titanic

The *Titanic* was launched on May 31, 1911 amidst a great fanfare. The enormous liner was the ultimate in sea-going luxury, displacing 66,000 tons, 104 feet high, 882·5 feet long, with two sets of 4-cylinder reciprocating engines producing 50,000 registered horsepower and a cruising speed of 24 to 25 knots. She could carry 3000 people in her luxuriously appointed three-class cabins. Her most publicized feature was her special construction, for she was divided into 16 separate watertight compartments. Her owners, the White Star Line, claimed that this made her virtually unsinkable.

Among her star attractions were expensive period furnishings, an exotically-decorated Turkish bath and the finest cuisine that money could buy. Not surprisingly, her maiden voyage prompted first-class bookings from the highest strata of society: countesses, lords, millionaires and industrial magnates made up a passenger list worth $250 million. Such an auspicious start to the *Titanic*'s career merited the presence on board of the President of the White Star Line himself, Bruce Ismay.

On April 10, 1912, the *Titanic* glided out of Southampton harbour bound for New York. The first few days of the voyage realized all the dreams of both owners and passengers: service was immaculate, dining and wining a positive delight, and the *beau monde* of Europe and America renewed old acquaintances and struck up new ones in an atmosphere of privileged security. Even their maids, valets and nannies received special attention from the seemingly endless army of ship's servants and had their own lounge on the 'C' deck.

Inflated self-confidence proved to be the *Titanic*'s disastrous end. This story of folly began on Sunday, April 14. The wireless operator, John Phillips, was busily sending out passengers' messages to Cape Race—radio was then still a novelty and the smart set made full use of it to let friends and relatives know their anticipated arrival time. In between the flood of personal cables, Phillips kept getting odd signals from other ships on the main transatlantic route ahead, from the *Caronia*, the *Baltic* and the *Californian*. There seemed to be large ice packs moving unusually far south from the chilly waters of the Arctic circle. About noon the *Baltic* tapped out: 'Have had moderate variable winds and clear fine weather since leaving. Greek steamer *Athenai* reports passing icebergs and large quantities of field ice today in Latitude 41·51° north, Longitude 49·52° west...'

In the first of a series of stupidities, this message somehow got into the hands of President Bruce Ismay, whose position on the liner alternated between *ex officio* Commodore and star guest, depending on the mood of the moment. Despite the significance of its contents, the message was shown to various lady passengers during the afternoon, but it did not get to the chartroom, where some sense might have been made of it, until 7.15pm. Meanwhile the *Titanic* proceeded on an unchanged course.

At about the same time, the temperature around the ship began to drop perceptibly from 43°F, to freezing point at about 10pm. Still no one in authority took the slightest notice. The radio officer could have taken action on a message intercepted around 7.30, from the *Californian* to the *Antillian*, again reporting three large icebergs. At 9.40, a third message was received by the *Titanic* from the *Mesaba*: 'Much heavy pack ice and a great number of large icebergs'. These two messages were never delivered to the bridge.

A blind disregard of all warning signs seemed to be leading the great liner into calamity. Only human fallibility can explain what happened when at 11pm the *Californian* directly contacted the *Titanic* to announce that it was totally hemmed in by ice and had stopped engines. John Phillips, by this time worn out with the day's work, could contain his irritation no longer. 'Shut up, shut up, I am busy!' he snapped back. His fatigue was evident to his right-hand man, second operator Bride, who came on duty at midnight, instead of at 2am, to relieve him.

The immediacy of the danger was beginning to dawn on Captain Edward Smith. By now the coldness of the air had prompted him to post six look-outs to watch for ice, but the passengers went to bed between 10 and 11pm unaware of any problem. Simultaneously, the *Titanic* drew so close that the ice-bound *Californian* could actually see her lights in the distance.

At 11.40, the mighty ship experienced a staggering collision with a giant iceberg. The look-outs had seen it, but the *Titanic* was upon the ice before the signal to reverse engines could have any effect. An enormous hole was ripped along one-third the length of the ship. Almost instantly the engine rooms began to fill with water.

Most people, including Bruce Ismay, only felt a 'slight judder', so massive was the bulk of the liner. But Ismay was experienced enough to sense that something untoward had taken place, so he got up and went to the bridge.

Meanwhile 3rd officer Charles Groves on the *Californian* saw the lights of the big ship go out,

Below *The much-publicized maiden voyage of the super-liner, the* Titanic. *Her owners, the White Star Line, claimed that she was 'unsinkable' due to her special construction of sixteen watertight steel compartments.*

but thought they had been turned off on purpose to give the hint to the few remaining wide-awake passengers. He could not know that the *Titanic* had swung sharply to port.

Those already in bed thought the whole incident was a huge joke. In one cabin, a man from Philadelphia had left his port-hole open and chunks of ice fell in on his bed as the iceberg slithered by. Other late-night drinkers in the first-class bar jumped from their seats to rush out and admire the floating hulks in the ocean, but soon retired to the coziness again and went on playing cards.

Down on the third-class deck, the humbler passengers were playing 'iceballs' and tripping back to their cabins with strange souvenirs: little cold lumps that soon melted in the warmth of the *Titanic*'s cabins.

Captain Smith knew the situation was serious. At 11.50 he ordered the radio room to send out immediate calls for help. Phillips, still there, tapped out the international 'CQD' and gave the ship's position, about 1500 miles from New York. Then Bride, just appearing to take over duty and hearing the momentous news, suggested they try the new 'SOS' signal. The *Titanic* made history as the first vessel in distress to use the new code.

A North German Lloyd steamer, the *Frankfurt*, answered first, followed by the Cunard Line *Carpathia*, some 58 miles away, and the Canadian Pacific vessel, called the *Mount Temple*.

Now the passengers began to realize something was wrong. The engines had stopped. The ship began to list frighteningly as the water relentlessly filled up room after room in the lower decks. Some of the third-class 'steerage' passengers, tucked away on the lower decks, awoke to find the floor of their cabins already awash.

Captain Smith knew the *Titanic* would sink. The water had risen 14 feet above the keel within the first ten minutes. The 'unsinkable' ship could keep afloat if any two of her 16 watertight compartments were flooded, even with three or four of her first five submerged. But the gash in her side meant that all five were filling rapidly. Even with automatic blocking mechanisms shutting off one compartment from another, the water would rise from the fifth up the stairways and through windows into the sixth, the seventh, the fifteenth in an unstoppable surge. At 12.05, the Captain ordered the lifeboats to be launched and in true-Brit old-world fashion, the word went out: 'Women and children first.'

Many stewards had to summon passengers still peacefully sleeping and get them up to the deck. There had been no lifeboat drill, and no practice at tying on life jackets, so there was bewilderment about where to go and what to do. Only the top-ranking officers and Bruce Ismay himself knew the awful truth about the lifeboat situation. There

Publicity pictures from London newspapers of the day.
Left *The ship's captain, E. J. Smith Cmdr, RNR.*
Top right *The Parisian cafe, in the style of a luxury hotel.*
Bottom right *For keep-fit fans, the latest equipment in a floating gymnasium.*

were only enough to take off just over half the passengers. The White Star Line had voluntarily exceeded the current legal requirements in this respect. Ship's regulations, worked out on a hopelessly inappropriate basis, called for the *Titanic* to carry boats for a maximum capacity of 962 people, whereas those supplied could carry 1178. On board that night were 2201 people, 1316 of whom were passengers. A third of those were female.

There was no raging storm, no fire and no mass panic, yet over half the people aboard the 'safest liner in the world' would be dead before the night was done.

Among the first-class passengers, husbands and fathers acted with admirable bravery, forcing their weeping wives and children to get into the lifeboats as the crew prepared them. Many ladies ran back to their cabins, seemingly oblivious of the urgency of the situation, to rescue fur coats, jewellery or other favoured trinkets. They presented an extraordinary picture, standing on the deck in lavish evening gowns, silken nightdresses and feathered hats.

Fifth officer Harold Lowe was busily ordering many of the women into Lifeboat Fourteen when Bruce Ismay approached, officiously telling everyone to hurry along and get off fast. Lowe lost his temper, and in spite of Ismay's high office, bellowed at him words to the effect 'If you'll get the hell out of the way, I'll be able to do something! You want me to lower away quickly? You'll have me drown the lot of them!' Other crew members looked shocked: Lowe would have had it when they all got to New York. But Ismay turned away without protest. He knew the true likelihood of survival. Lifeboat Fourteen got off with 55 people —one of the fuller boats. There were damning

scenes of selfishness among others escaping the now rapidly sinking ship. Number One was lowered with only 12 people, when its capacity was 40. Sir Cosmo and Lady Duff Gordon, her secretary, two Americans, six stokers and one of the ice look-out men, Symons, made up the load. Number Six went down at 12.55, Number Three at 1am, Number Eight at 1.10am. Number Five shoved off with 40 people, when it could have held 65.

The figures prove conclusively that the first-class passengers were looked after in preference to the lower classes. Only four of the first-class women died, three by choice, when they refused to be separated from their husbands. One of these was Mrs Isador Straus, wife of an American millionaire. She and her husband sat calmly side by side and waited for the ship to sink.

Of the 93 second-class women, 15 survived; out of 179 third-class, only 81 were saved. At one stage, the doors between the third-class quarters and the upper decks were locked to prevent people from surging on to the upper levels, but the passengers either knocked them down or pushed the seamen guards out of the way.

The men in first-class probably had little idea of the lack of assistance given to the 'lower order'. For the most part they observed 'women and children first' in strict honour. Benjamin Guggenheim and his valet disappeared to their cabins and returned in evening dress, once they saw the women off and knew there was no hope for themselves. They sat down in splendour to await their fate. Howard Case, a London oil executive, waved goodbye to his lady friends and was last seen leaning against the top deck sea rail, nonchalantly lighting a cigarette.

By the time most of the first-class women had got off the ship, the third-class passengers were still struggling to find their way up from the lower decks. Those aristocrats and magnates left contemplating their doom were astonished to see clusters of yet more women and children emerging from below. Some braver ones crawled up the escape ladders from the well deck aft; others found passageways through corridors rapidly filling with water and clambered over the side of the ship into the water.

While chaos reigned above, most of the crew below still had no thought of leaving the sinking ship. Between midnight and 2am, a desperate attempt was under way to pump boiler room 5 dry. Just when it looked as if the men would succeed, the entire bulkhead between rooms 5 and 6 gave way and the whole area was again flooded with icy water. One man managed to clamber up the escape ladder: another turned to help a mate with a broken leg and disappeared into the rising tide.

Radio man Phillips continued at his post frantically tapping out 'SOS' and details of the ship's position. Bride, the second in command, strapped on Phillips' life jacket without disturbing his work. Around 2.18 he had to fight off a desperate attacker who stole up behind the radio man, ready to rip the jacket off his back.

Finally the Captain gave the last order: 'Every man for himself', and the crew were freed from their responsibilities to the magnificent liner. The end was fast approaching. On the starboard deck one of the small collapsible lifeboats, 'C' was the last to be launched. Four crewmen and 45 passengers got in, including President Ismay. He was later criticized severely for saving himself when

he must have known that not all the passengers, not even all women and children, had got off.

1503 people were left to go down with the *Titanic*. Those lifeboats that got away safely could have picked up many of the wretched victims floundering all around in the cold ocean, but few stopped or turned back to pick up more people. Fifth Officer Lowe made the noblest effort. As his lifeboat approached four others, numbers 10, 12 and 4, and collapsible craft D, he gave orders to lash them together. He then circled around to pick up anyone he could find in the sea. He only saved four.

In Lifeboat Five, the women stoutly refused to accept an officer's suggestion that they row around searching, although they could not have been more than 300 yards from several swimmers whose cries could be heard across the waves. In Number Six, the situation was reversed: several first-class ladies implored their seaman to go back but he refused. In sorrow and silence they took turns rowing about four miles before they neared the rescue ships answering the SOS. It was a shameful episode. Of approximately 1500, only 13 people were pulled out of the water by 18 lightly loaded boats.

About 2.20am, the *Titanic* began her final dive into the Atlantic. At an almost perpendicular angle, she slid down into the waves. The ship's band, had stoically played a selection of ragtime tunes through the abandonment, but turned to an Episcopal hymn, *Autumn* (some say it was *Nearer My God to Thee*). As everything inside the vessel broke loose, there was an awe-inspiring roar, followed by silence. In the vortex created by the sinking *Titanic*, people in the sea were sucked under; others were flung off the decks and rails as she toppled over. That was the last of her. The boatloads of survivors turned their backs and pulled away into the night.

Aid was not long in arriving. Captain Rostron of the *Carpathia* had been so shocked by the SOS picked up from the *Titanic* that he radioed back to find out if it was 'absolutely certain' the liner was in distress. Once confirmed, the news was acted upon with all speed. The captain later confessed: 'When I saw the ice I had steamed through during the night, I shuddered and could only think that some other hand than mine was on the helm that night.'

One by one the lifeboats were sighted: between 4.45 and 8.30 they bobbed alongside the Cunard Liner, 705 survivors in all, including Ismay. He retired immediately to the ship's doctor's cabin and remained there until the ship docked in New York.

Meanwhile the *Californian* had seen the distress rockets sent up by the sinking ship, and her captain realized that those lights that had been spotted earlier were from the same vessel. At 5.40am, the wireless operator was summoned and

This page, above The Carpathia *braved the ice floes with a dramatic dash to reach survivors.*
Below *Survivors huddle on the deck of the rescue ship.*
Above right *The cause of the 'unsinkable' liner's destruction was a huge iceberg like this. Only about one ninth of its bulk is above water; the rest is hidden treacherously below the surface.*
Below right *There was no proper lifeboat drill on board the* Titanic, *unlike this scene where all the passengers escape a liner fire. Even if the ship had been better organized, many would still have died, for the* Titanic *carried only enough lifeboats for just over half the total number of passengers.*

ordered to open the radio channels and find out what had happened. Their horror can be imagined when it became clear that the greatest liner in the world had gone down less than 20 miles away, and they had known nothing about it.

In New York, news was received with equally stunned amazement. The White Star Line's offices were beseiged with anxious relatives, from the wealthiest to the poorest, wanting news. None came from the *Carpathia* until she docked four days later. 30,000 people waited on the water-front.

Class distinction was maintained right through the aftermath of the disaster. The *New York American* newspaper devoted most of its coverage to millionaire John Jacob Astor, one of the first-class men who sat calmly waiting until he went down with the *Titanic*. The other 1800 lost were mentioned in a brief note at the foot of the front page.

At the Boards of Enquiry held in the USA and Britain, few witnesses from third-class were even called, let alone given fair attention, in spite of their accusations that they had been prevented from going up to the boat deck. Discrimination extended to 'foreigners': so many rude remarks were made by witnesses about the disorderly and cowardly behaviour of men passengers from below—'probably Italians, or some foreign nationality' as one put it, that the Italian Ambassador in New York demanded an official apology.

Although Bruce Ismay was severely chastized for saving himself by the American board, he was absolved by the British one, which concluded: 'Had he not jumped in he would merely have added one more life, namely his own, to the number of those lost.'

Blame was laid against the Captain and senior officers for failure to take notice of the four ice warnings that had been received. The Captain of the *Californian* was criticized for not going to the aid of the *Titanic*, though she was ice-bound and had her radio closed down for the night.

Worst of all was the lifeboat situation. Badly equipped, poorly positioned for launching and totally insufficient in number, they were the main reason for the loss of so many lives. The White Star Line was not legally to blame, but Bruce Ismay felt the moral burden, for he retired to Ireland soon after, living in virtual isolation until his death in 1937.

Could the *Titanic* disaster be repeated? It did bring about major reforms in passenger ship regulations. The required number of lifeboats was revised to cope with the maximum possible load. Boat drill became a rule. Perhaps more important, ship's radios must now remain open night and day to prevent a repeat of the *Californian*'s failure to respond. But there is no easy remedy for the most unforgivable aspect of the *Titanic* disaster: the disgraceful selfishness displayed by many of the survivors. Even in today's somewhat more egalitarian society, there might be some who would row away to safety, ignoring the cries of the helpless in an ice-bound sea.

May 22, 1915
Train crash at
Quintinshill

Quintinshill Junction is unimportant as railway posts go, situated ten miles north of Carlisle, near Gretna Junction on the English–Scottish border. There were no peculiar weather conditions on the morning of May 22, 1915. It should have been a perfectly normal turn of duty for the two signalmen whose sole responsibility was manning the signal box there.

There are two main tracks at Quintinshill, one to the north, one to the south. In addition there are two 'loops': lay-by tracks on each side of the main line where trains can wait, parallel to the up and down lines.

In the early hours of that morning, two express trains had left Euston Station, London at 11.45

and midnight, and were both half an hour late by the time they neared Carlisle. As a result, another northbound train, a local from Carlisle, was sent to Quintinshill before the expresses, reversing its normal order. Because it provided a connection for Edinburgh and Glasgow at Beattock for passengers from Moffat, it had to keep to its schedule, and it was sent as far as Quintinshill so it would not lose too much time. There, it would wait in one of the loops until the expresses had gone through and could then proceed on its journey without much delay.

There was another unusual occurrence, unofficial and altogether secret. The night duty signalman, Meakin, was supposed to finish duty at

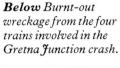

Below Burnt-out wreckage from the four trains involved in the Gretna Junction crash.

6am. But when he heard that the local from Carlisle was going to stop at Quintinshill, he stayed on the job, knowing that his relief, signalman Tinsley, would take advantage of an easy ride and come on the local from his home at Gretna Junction. Meakin covered up for his friend's late arrival by noting down all train movements and other messages received on a scrap of paper from 6 o'clock onwards. When Tinsley arrived, he would copy them into the official register, so that a different handwriting would appear at the right time. The system had worked without mishap several times before. After all, Quintinshill was not an important post.

The situation soon became more complicated. At 6.14am, Meakin saw the 4.50 goods train from Carlisle approaching. He arranged for this to wait in the down loop at the side of the main line. At 6.34 he signalled an empty coal train from the north into the lay-by on the up side. There were now only two lines of track free. With an alarming lack of foresight, Meakin instructed the local, just arrived, to switch to the up main line. It stood only 65 yards from his signal box, steaming merrily and awaiting further orders.

From the signal box at Gretna Junction, Meakin received word of the first approaching Scottish express, speeding on its way to make up for lost time. At this point, Tinsley appeared in the box to take over the daytime shift. As they exchanged a few words of greeting, another message flashed through, saying that a special troop train, carrying a regiment of the 7th Royal Scots to Liverpool, would soon be coming through Quintinshill. In other words, it was heading directly for the local, standing on the up main line. Neither Meakin nor Tinsley seemed perturbed by the quantity of early morning traffic coming their way. Meakin, in no hurry to rush off, settled down to read the morning newspaper supplied by Tinsley when he arrived. Two railwaymen from the goods trains parked in the loops appeared in the box to have a chat. Tinsley began writing up the entries he'd missed from 6 o'clock onwards in the big book, the Train Register.

Although the copying-up procedure was highly irregular, in this instance it meant that both Meakin and Tinsley were in a position to see their fatal mistake. Meakin should have realized that the local was blocking the line on which the troop train would be travelling. Even if he had a momentary lapse and overlooked it, Tinsley should have realized the error as he was copying up the entries.

In retrospect some spell seems to have been cast over these men to prevent commonsense from operating, for they were given yet another chance to remedy the confusion. 'Collars', supplied by the Railway Company, were to be dropped over the handles of the signal controls whenever a train blocked a main through-line to prevent a signalman from throwing the lever and giving an 'all-clear': no other train could pass on to that section of track while the collar was in place.

The fireman of the local came to check on the

position of his train, obediently following Rule 55 of railway regulations:

'If a train is held for more than three minutes, the fireman should visit the nearest box and confirm that the signalman is aware of the train's presence, and that proper precautions are taken'.

Fireman Hutchinson did not notice that the collar was not in place on the signal controls, nor did his arrival jog the memory of either Meakin or Tinsley about the position of the local and its now-impatient passengers.

At 6.38 Tinsley gave the signal for the approaching Scottish express from Euston. At 6.42 he gave the signal for the southbound troop train. Two minutes later the troop train, travelling very fast downhill on a gradient of 1-in-200, ploughed into the engine of the stationary local. The troop train was pulled by a four-coupled bogie express; the local by a No. 907, a heavy 4-6-0. The impact was tremendous. The coupling on the local broke, shooting the passenger carriages backwards for 136 yards. The engine ground back along the track for 40 yards and finally stopped half off the line, with its tender lying across the other main line. The troop train too turned sideways, blocking both tracks. The coaches of the troop train, packed with soldiers, were smashed to smithereens. Like many early 20th-century trains, the superstructures were made of wood. They splintered like matchsticks with the force of the impact. One carriage hurtled into the air, sailed over the engine and smashed to the ground in front of it. In one moment, a train 213 yards long was squashed,

Above Some of the 227 injured in the multi-collision received immediate aid in a field lying alongside the track.
Overleaf Only 52 men of the 7th Battalion of the Royal Scots were able to answer roll call the day after the crash. The other members of the unit, which had been 500-strong, were either dead or injured.

concertina-like, to a mere 67 yards long.

Injuries to the soldiers were appalling. Those who were stunned, dazed, but able, struggled to escape and help their comrades. As defenceless men began to think of rescue and safety, the Scottish express ploughed along the northbound line. Too late, Tinsley and Meakin realized what was going to happen. All the railwaymen who had been in the box ran hysterically along the track in a vain attempt to warn the express. One minute after the first collision, the express, weighing 600 tons, headed straight into the wreckage. The driver just had time to apply his brakes for a full emergency stop on the first of the express's two four-coupled bogies. But the sheer weight of the train bore it forward. It hit the troop train and drove its tender right through the wagons of the goods train standing on the down loop.

Survivors from the first collision had no chance. Within seconds the coal supply on the troop train ignited, probably due to the gaslight fixtures in the carriages, and flames lapped wildly over the mountain of iron and wood. Vain efforts were made to control the blaze with water pumped from a stream running through a nearby farm. Passengers who had escaped from the last carriages of the express train and the few soldiers left alive could do nothing to help those trapped

inside the carriages as the heat of the fire rapidly became intense and drove them back. Instead of supplying water to quench the blaze, the little farm became an improvized morgue for the bodies that could be extricated from the tangled mass of wreckage. Those who survived were laid in the flat field beside the train line to the east.

Most of the victims were Scottish soldiers on the way to the trenches in France. Because it was wartime, news coverage was limited and tried to hit a note of morale-boosting, even in the midst of unprecedented loss. The Quintinshill crash was the worst in British history, with 227 dead and 246 injured. But the newspapers concealed the horror under drum-beating: of the soldiers, it was reported, 'all had been in high spirits at the prospect of going to the front . . . They were men of magnificent physique, and they fought their road through the wreckage as though they had been called upon to storm a German trench.' But Private E Donald of the 2nd Life Guards who was travelling in the London express said soldiers 'who had been at the front said none of the scenes they had seen in the trenches were as bad'. Within days, the newspapers carried reports that a new regiment was to be raised immediately to replace the Quintinshill contingent at the front.

Hundreds of sightseers flocked to the site on

the Whitsun holiday that unfortunately came close after the disaster. There was plenty to see. The fire had blazed steadily all through the night after the crash. The Carlisle Fire Brigade had arrived at 10 that morning and struggled all day to control it, but by 9 o'clock the following day, 15 coaches of the troop train, four coaches of the express, five goods wagons and all the coal had gone up in flames. Even after breakdown gangs had been hard at work all day, a 100-yard stretch of track was still littered with débris—wheels retained their shape, strangely, but engine parts were distorted into unrecognizable lumps of gnarled metal.

Meakin and Tinsley were solely responsible for Quintinshill. Given safety precautions in existence at the time, they failed to do their duty. Both were sentenced to jail, the first for 18 months, the second for three years. But the memory of their failure was punishment enough. Both men had nervous breakdowns and were released after a year.

There were other precautions that could have been taken. Wooden superstructures are extremely unsafe especially for passenger transport. The troop train was made entirely of wood, even its under-frames. Gas lighting is extremely hazardous and probably made the fire catch more quickly and spread more energetically. There was also some doubt about the availability of crash equipment. The Scots soldiers had their own tools wagons coupled to their train; these were used to free survivors trapped in the wreckage. Without this chance event, many more lives would have been lost for lack of vital equipment.

Nowadays, important junctions are protected by being 'track circuited' at the joints. A section of track is insulated from adjoining sections. An electrically-operated switch is kept closed by a low-voltage current passing through the rails at all times. When a train runs over this part of the track, it 'short-circuits' the current, so that the switch opens. Even if the current fails by accident, the effect is the same. The movement of the switch is transmitted to the signal box: no other train can go on to that section of the line until it is cleared. A series of these circuits could effectively plot the progress of a train for its entire journey, although the system is too expensive to install everywhere.

That was the tragedy of Quintinshill. A small, unimportant junction would probably not have qualified for such sophisticated techniques. To work properly, the Quintinshill Junction depended on human skill, a quality all too absent on that May morning.

CANADA

NOVA
SCOTIA

Halifax

ATLANTIC
OCEAN

December 7, 1917
Explosion in Halifax harbour

Below Richmond, Nova Scotia, lay in ruins after the Mont Blanc *explosion.* **Inset** *The Belgian relief ship* Imo *collided with the ammunition ship.*

The French freighter *Mont Blanc* picked up a dangerous cargo in New York: 5000 tons of high explosives and combustible materials. The 3121-ton vessel was loaded with TNT, picric acid, gun cotton and barrels of benzene, ready for shipment to Europe. In December 1917 such supplies were vitally necessary for the war against the Germans—so necessary that the *Mont Blanc* was under orders to sail north to Halifax harbour, Nova Scotia, Canada, to meet up with the British cruiser, HMS *High Flyer*, which would lead the convoy safely across the Atlantic.

The *High Flyer* was already waiting in Halifax harbour when the *Mont Blanc* steamed in at about 9 o'clock on Thursday, December 6. Thin patchy fog made visibility a little difficult, but with a pilot on board, there was no cause for undue worry.

The harbour is six miles long with a breadth of about one mile, and affords secure deep-water anchorage at all times of the day, whatever the tide, for the largest ships afloat. But there is a point in the passage, called 'The Narrows', where the harbour slims down to a half-mile-wide channel. On the south shore lies the Richmond section of Halifax; on the north, the town of Dartmouth.

The pilot suddenly gave a mighty blast on his horn, for a ship was bearing down directly on the *Mont Blanc*—the outward-sailing Belgian relief ship, *Imo*. *Mont Blanc*'s captain gives an on-the-spot account of what happened next:

'The *Imo* signalled that she was coming to port which would bring her to the same side with us. We were keeping to starboard and could not understand what the *Imo* meant, but kept our course, hoping that she would come down as she should on the starboard side, which would keep her on the Halifax side of the harbour.

'. . . Then we put the rudder hard aport to try to pass the *Imo* before she should come on to us. At the same time the *Imo* reversed engines. As she was light, without cargo, the reverse brought her around slightly to port, her bow towards our starboard. As a collision was then inevitable, we held so that she would be struck forward of the hold where the picric acid substance, which would not explode, was stored, rather than have her strike where the TNT was stored'.

There was an almighty crash as the *Imo* sank deep into the *Mont Blanc*. Then, she reversed off desperately, while the sailors aboard the ammunition ship made a few frenzied efforts to scupper the *Mont Blanc* before the deadly cargo did any damage. But they soon realized that fire had already broken out where some of the benzene load had spilt on impact. A quick order came to abandon ship, and the crew obeyed, struggling to lower lifeboats and row as fast and as far away as they could.

On Pier 8, where the *Mont Blanc* should have docked, the fire alarm was raised. Halifax's one and only fire-fighting unit set out at full speed from the town, heading for the harbour. The Richmond telegraph operator Vincent Coleman also saw the fire and mistakenly telegraphed: 'A munition ship is on fire and is making for Pier 8. Good-bye.' He then hurried off to find his newly-wed wife.

The *Mont Blanc* crew got to shore and ran into the nearby woods. Suddenly it became clear that the ship was an enormous floating bomb, liable to explode at any second. People started to swarm out of dockside factories, offices and houses and scramble up the steep-sided cliff towards the historic Citadel building, Halifax's old fortress.

Another British ammunition ship, the *Pictou*, was already moored at Pier 8, and within seconds of the realization that the *Mont Blanc* would blow, she too was completely abandoned. Only the *High Flyer* took preventive action: the cruiser sent a boarding party in a launch with instructions to get to the *Mont Blanc* and sink her before anything terrible could happen.

But happen it did: about 15 minutes after the collision, the *Mont Blanc* drifting slowly towards the wharf, exploded in one enormous blast. An eye witness, William Barton, breakfasting at the Halifax Hotel, looked out at the scene in stunned realization:

'In ten seconds it was all over. A low rumbling, an earthquake shock, with everything vibrating, then an indescribable noise, followed by the fall of plaster, and the smashing of glass. A cry went up: "A German bomb".'

Through the smashed doors, survivors streamed out of the hotel and joined the panic-stricken multitude swarming up the harbour hillside to safety. The very geography of the place made the explosion all the more destructive, for the deep, high-sided channel contained the impact.

Damage to both life and property was immense. The blast was felt over 60 miles away. Half the city lay in ruins. The Intercolonial Railway Station, a brick and stone structure in downtown Halifax, was totally flattened, killing crowds of people waiting for trains on platforms or already seated in carriages. Schools too suffered great loss of life because at that hour—9.15am—everyone was assembled to begin lessons. Of 550 children in the Halifax area alone, only seven survived. The total number of people who died has never been established exactly, but conservative estimates put it at 1200, while others believe it may have been as great as 4000.

In the immediate harbour area, a large sugar-refining factory, the pier, the fire engine and its crew and almost all other buildings were completely destroyed. One hundred workers are known to have died in the refining plant.

The other area to suffer the greatest effect of the explosion was Richmond, across the harbour, because most of the houses were built of wood and clustered into narrow streets. The Richmond telegraph operator who ran for his wife was one of those people who died. After the blast, the second great danger, fire, broke out here and in other parts of Halifax, and 25,000 people were made homeless.

Among the survivors, 5000 gathered in the open city common and were saved from further danger of explosion by the flooding of the naval ammunition depot near the Narrows, and by the courageous action of the Marine superintendent, J W Harrison, who got aboard the British ammunition ship *Pictou* and opened the sea valves. He set the vessel adrift, with water hoses playing over the decks, and within minutes the ship and all her cargo sank.

The Richmond telegraph operator's message was received in Moncton and St John. From the first a special train left at full speed, as early as 9.30, loaded with doctors, nurses, Red Cross helpers and all necessary medical supplies. Several more trains followed to take some of the homeless to shelter and to bring fire-fighting equipment.

The rescue effort was hampered by appalling weather conditions, for the morning fog worsened into driving snow and freezing temperatures. Wounded people lying amid the brick, rubble, shattered glass and charred wood had the added threat of exposure forced upon them. Electricity supplies were disrupted by the blast, so relief workers had to struggle in the increasing gloom, searching for the injured, who were rapidly becoming indistinguishable mounds in the snow among the dead.

On the outskirts of Halifax, people felt the tremor of the blast and saw the glass in their windows splinter and fly. The news came through to a girls' school, St Vincent's Academy, when a locomotive driven at full speed by one engineer arrived. He cried for help, bandages, clothes, anything, and the girls set about tearing up their uniforms to make dressings for the injured.

The snow had one beneficial effect: it suc-

ceeded in damping down the fires that had broken out. By afternoon, the danger had passed, but only wreck and ruin remained. A 2½-square mile area in the city centre was completely flattened.

Halifax city militia took command and declared martial law. More trains arrived with medical supplies and doctors and nurses from Boston and New York. All remaining public buildings, such as the Academy of Music, were opened to house the injured and the homeless. In the city common, the troops put up 500 tents for themselves and let women and children move into their barracks.

The explosion had the effect of bringing home to Canadians the full horrors of war. Previously the battles in Europe had been far away and only the movement of troops and war supplies reminded them of the dreadful struggle taking place in Europe. But *The Times* of London, ever mindful of the need to keep morale high at home took the opportunity to publicize the opinion of Lieutenant-Colonel Good of Fredericton, who said that he had never seen such a sight on the battlefields of France. 'All that could be seen for a great circumference were burning buildings, great mounds of iron and brick in the streets, and dead bodies'—anything that minimized the horror of the trenches was welcome to a British newspaper. But in Canada, unaccustomed to war on its doorstep, the disaster of Halifax harbour was doubly shocking: unexpected and unimagined. That was why the hotel guest thought the blast must have come from a German bomb. Nothing but a full-scale war offensive could explain the black pall of smoke that hung in the air—it must have been aerial attack. But, as the newspapers recorded, only 12 soldiers were killed at Halifax harbour. Thousands of civilians died; 8000 or more were injured and 3000 homes were destroyed. The true cause was not a planned act of aggression, but a momentary unthinking confusion over ships' signals.

JAPAN

Tokyo

PACIFIC
OCEAN

September 1, 1923
The Tokyo Earthquake

Tokyo has often been afflicted by earthquakes, yet the superb location of the city on the mouth of the Sumida River, facing an enormous natural bay, has made it a centre of habitation for 4000 years. In the feudal era it was the beautiful imperial city of Edo, full of castles and moats; some of its old palaces and temples still stood at the beginning of the 20th century as reminders of the city's long cultural history and economic importance. But in 1923 Tokyo and the neighbouring port of Yokohama were devastated by Japan's worst earthquake, which almost wiped the ancient city and its people out of existence.

Because the warm mild climate and the Japanese style of living encourage houses built in flimsy structures out of simple wood panelling, the effect of the tremors were far worse than in San Francisco. The houses were simply flattened into firewood. The death toll was also infinitely greater. The earthquake happened in the middle of the day when the streets were full of workers going to lunch, and the coastal areas were

Below Yokohama, Japan's largest seaport, serving nearby Tokyo, immediately after the earthquake. Eighty percent of the buildings in the city were destroyed.

thronged with holiday-makers enjoying late summer sun and picnics in the parks.

At 11.58 on September 1, there was a violent tremor, followed by a second and a third. Seven prefectures of Tokyo were completely destroyed: Tokyo centre, Kanagawa, Shizuoka, Chiba, Saitama, Yamanashi and Ibaraki. Yokohama was also wiped out. The whole bay area was devastated.

In some areas, the land shifted up as much as eight or nine feet. The upheavals and depressions ran in a line from north to west and south to east between the Manazuru Peninsula and the Boso Peninsula, across Sagami Bay, in a direct path south of Tokyo itself. The most remarkable alteration in the landscape took place south of Yokohama, at the foot of the peninsula forming one of the arcs of Tokyo Bay. Just off Misaki, right at the tip, stands the island of Jogashima. The land there surged upwards with such force that the entire channel between the island and the mainland was laid bare, revealing hundreds of shell-covered rocks on what had been the ocean floor. During the first few days after the earthquake, land levels altered at the rate of two feet per day, until the final settlement stood five feet above the pre-quake height.

A second natural phenomenon caused instant heavy casualties: a *tsunami*, or tidal wave, lunged out of the sea at Atami on Sagami Bay, west of Yokohama, destroying 150 houses along the front and carrying off 60 people. The length of the giant tsunami from crest to crest may be more than 100 miles, and their height as little as two or three feet in open sea. They can pass through the ocean at speeds of up to 600 miles per hour. As they near the coast, they slow down, building up greater height, until they thunder on to the shore. So great is the force of a tsunami that, before it arrives, it causes the normal water line to recede dramatically or forces it forward to half again its usual height. Tsunamis are lethal; by the time an eye-witness has seen one build up on its run for the shore, it is too late for him to escape. The wave will overwhelm anyone and anything near enough to see it. The most common causes are vertical shifting in the sea bed, submarine avalanches or landslides on the ocean floor—or extended earthquake tremors. The first and third explanations might apply to the Sagami Bay disaster. At the time it was thought that the sea bed below the bay had sunk by as much as 40 fathoms, or 240 feet. Vertical displacement caused several waves along the coast, washing away many villages west of Tokyo and Yokohama.

The number of people who died in Tokyo as a direct result of the earthquake was comparatively few. Even so, the figures are high. A giant tower of the Asakusa temple crushed 700 people when it tumbled. Two great hotels in Yokohama, the Grand and the Oriental, collapsed almost instantly. In the rubble and the fire that followed 180 people, including 100 foreigners, died. Six hundred more were buried in a railway tunnel.

Below *Devastation in a Yokohama street.*

As in San Francisco, even greater calamity came with a monstrous conflagration that soon overwhelmed both Tokyo and Yokohama. All the water mains were dislocated and all electric cables snapped, so there was little hope of immediate aid when hundreds of small fires began to flare up within an instant of the third, and strongest, tremor. Most people had already lit their little charcoal and wood burners to make midday tea and rushed out of their houses in panic without thought of fire. The wind lifted, and as the heat of the fires increased, cyclones formed in the low-pressure atmosphere. Soon these swirling, circling mini-tornados swept across the city, spreading the fires uncontrollably.

By late afternoon an unusually strong cyclone built up in the northern part of the Sumida River and swept down its banks throwing small boats several feet in the air. It whirled over the burning school building at Kuramaye and sucked up a mass of flames, smoke and burning splinters. At Honjo, directly in its path, terrified refugees had gathered for safety, away from their shattered homes, in the grounds of a large clothing depot. The cyclone roared over the enclosure, setting it alight and suffocating everyone inside. All 40,000 perished in the blaze.

Downtown Tokyo presented a scene of devastation and confusion. Violent winds blew flames first this way, then that. There was no water to fight the fire. People ran screaming through the streets as quake-shaken buildings toppled about

them. Looting, arson, jail-breaks and other forms of civil disorder gripped the citizens in what the official report described as a 'reign of terror'. The police were completely unequal to the task of restoring calm. One strange aspect of reaction was that Korean residents in Tokyo (Japan had annexed their country in 1910) were somehow blamed for the violence and were so energetically persecuted that eventually special sanctuaries were set up for them at Narashino in Chiba Prefecture. More than 3000 Koreans fled for their lives.

The citizens of Tokyo gathered in the open spaces outside the Imperial Palace grounds and various other palaces and gardens throughout the day. Streets were jammed with anxious families pushing carts, carrying wicker baskets crammed with precious articles and clutching their children. Luckily as evening approached the air did not cool to a sharpness. They spent the night under the open sky without exposure. But food and water were severe problems. The army immediately donated a huge store of rice from a military provision depot at Etchujima, but before the city authorities could organize its collection, the building and its goods were destroyed by fire. Feverish activity began the same day on repairing broken water mains, and Tokyo was back on a limited supply by September 3, just two days later. Meanwhile, military vehicles and municipal water carts went round the refugee parks doling out small cupfuls to the thousands parched with thirst from

Below Many of Tokyo's ancient monuments were destroyed.
Overleaf Panic, looting and a total breakdown of law and order immobilized Tokyo in the aftermath of the 'quake.

the fire and smoke that surrounded them.

The panic grew so out of hand that martial law was officially declared on September 2. The Imperial Guard, the First Division of the Army and several infantry troops and engineer corps were sent to the area to help the police in organizing restoration of peace and order. The same day an emergency requisition ordinance went out and all supplies of food, fuel, medicines, vehicles and ships came under the control of a central Emergency Relief Bureau. The aim was to stop blackmarketeering and share resources in the best possible manner.

In Tokyo, every major building was destroyed: 17 libraries, including that of the Imperial Palace, 151 Shinto shrines, 633 Buddhist temples and 202 Christian churches or missions were laid flat. Not one house escaped undamaged from the earthquake or the fire. In Tokyo Prefecture alone 59,000 people died, 10,900 were missing and 8700 were seriously injured.

Yokohama suffered equally severe devastation. It is situated in Kanagawa province, for which official records of the dead stood at 58,000, 21,000 of whom were in the port. Over 6000 people were injured and over 2000 lost. The total number of people killed or seriously injured in the whole region came to 156,693.

Yokohama had waked on September 1 to a rainy, gusty day, but by 10am the skies cleared and the crowds came out. Ten minutes before noon the earthquake hit. Mr Morioka, the Chief of Police, immediately set up headquarters in the central park and ordered out the fire brigades. He set out on a tour of inspection. The Customs House was ablaze, but nothing could be done as all available fire hydrants were broken. Large numbers of dead littered the streets. Survivors rushed towards the Park, but it had been turned into a quagmire by a burst water main and great rifts had appeared in the ground.

Along the river embankments and on city slopes, houses had slithered into the water. All roads were cracked and all bridges destroyed. By mid-afternoon Yokohama, like Tokyo, was in the grip of a conflagration made worse by high winds. At the docks, the warehouses at Nakamura, filled with explosives, roared and burst apart. People attempting to escape in tiny boats in the bay were soon caught as oil seeping over the water ignited.

When the police chief got back to Prefectural Building, which had survived the 'quake, he found it crammed with refugees but in imminent danger of catching fire from a blazing silk factory next door. He gathered up the people intending to head towards the Park, but now the streets were blocked with fire. The little crowd turned this way and that until it got to the quayside. In his own recollection, Mr Morioka described how the ground literally opened and shut in great cracks, so intense were the aftershocks that hit the region.

The crowd reached the quay, and the police chief had little alternative but to plunge into the oily water and swim to a nearby launch. He

Above More lives were lost in the fires that broke out after the tremors than were taken by the earthquake itself. Five hundred girls perished in this cotton spinning factory at Koyama.

ordered it to go to nearby ships, including the *Korea Maru,* and to pass the word to all bigger vessels to come alongside the quay and take off survivors. Thousands of people, backing on to the water's edge from the flaming city, were rescued by the combined efforts of the local ships. Morioka used the radio on the *Korea Maru* to send out one of the first messages about the earthquake to reach neighbouring areas:

'Today at noon a great earthquake occurred and was immediately followed by a conflagration which has changed the whole city into a sea of fire causing countless casualties. All facilities of traffic have been destroyed and communications cut off. We have neither water nor food. For God's sake, send relief at once.'

Without hesitation all cargo ships in the port of Yokohama offered their loads to help feed the starving survivors. When the news was received by the central government, two warships, *Yamashiro* and *Kasuga,* were dispatched to help.

Such was the confusion in the port, in particular on the old wharves leading into the main bay, that many ships were jammed into their moorings, and soon caught fire from sparks carried over from shoreline buildings. Many sailors jumped overboard in the burning sea or rushed on to the quayside where they soon lost their way in panic. By the end of the day the harbour master, who had been badly injured in the head, somehow

found his way to the port and got out to the *Korea Maru.* He soon set about reorganizing the berthing of the ships lying higgledy-piggledy all over the harbour.

Two great landmarks of Yokohama were destroyed by the disaster. The first was the long customs house pier that jutted far out into the harbour. This and the newly-built quayside provided deep mooring for liners coming to Japan from all corners of the world. Now the pier hung like a crumbling dead snake, pushed this way and that by the force of the 'quake.

The other monument was the Daijingu shrine, noted for its lovely groves of plum trees that blossom in February. Nothing remained but charred tree trunks and stone debris. The only reminder of former beauty was a small bronze statue of Li Kamon-no-Kami, a former minister-president who had done much to promote Yokohama as a prosperous centre of foreign commerce. The whole statue, pedestal and all, was completely turned round from north to east, as if moved by a giant hand.

Considering the total effect of devastation on Tokyo and Yokohama, it is a wonder that they ever recovered, but the energy that had turned the area into one of the world's greatest ports and commercial centres soon reasserted itself. The first news of the disaster reached Osaka on the evening of the first day and through the night the Army Aviation Headquarters sent planes to reconnoitre the area and report exactly what was happening and what relief was immediately needed.

Within the next few days a novel method of communication helped Tokyo to get the outside equipment and services so desperately needed. A special carrier pigeon corps was organized by the army and formed a dispatch service between Nikko (where the Imperial villa was situated), Chiba, Osaka, Odawara and other towns nearby.

The worst problem was housing and shelter. After a week, there were still 13,000 people in the Imperial Palace grounds, 5200 near Tokyo Station, 5600 in Hibiya Park, and 2000 near Municipal headquarters. The army lent tents and put up barracks to provide temporary accommodation, but the government report on the earthquake noted that every effort was being made to get rid of them as soon as possible. Within weeks, because they were hurriedly built and took in refugees irrespective of their means and occupations, there were wide differences in the condition of occupants, leaving much to be desired from both morale and sanitary points of view.

Disease was a further hazard after the earthquake, with epidemics of dysentery, typhoid and other illnesses causing the death of another 3705 people.

But the Japanese spirit began to pull the citizens of Tokyo through. First, railway and steamship companies volunteered transport to take away refugees. Two million left by September 16, easing the burden on the emergency network. From September 6 large supplies of food began to arrive in the city from the surrounding country-

side, helping to restore the normal routine of family life. Street markets re-opened and mothers could go shopping. For two weeks after the earthquake, what little public transport could operate was run free for all citizens, but the administrators did not allow easy charity to continue for long. After the 16th, passengers had to produce a special certificate to prove they were 'earthquake sufferers' to get the concession.

These moves helped the citizens to regain their sense of place and independence. Their worst problem was insurance, because nearly all shopkeepers, house owners and business owners had overlooked a standard clause in most local insurance schemes, exempting the protected party in case of earthquake. The government finally stepped in and set up aid schemes so most people could claim at least enough to make a fresh start. In the USA, President Coolidge and the Red Cross began a fund with a $5,000,000 target figure; within a few days twice that amount was received and donated. Other nations sent money, ships, supplies and medical teams in the months that followed.

Tokyo's recovery was impressive. It faced fresh calamity in the heavy air-raids made by American bombers in World War II, but by 1970, its population had increased to 22,000,000 in the urban area, and it has become the centre of Japan's financial and industrial life, overtaking Osaka. But the threat of devastation by earthquake is ever-present and seemingly without any hope of a cure.

Above *A tidal wave or 'tsunami' swept into Sagami Bay, west of Yokohama, destroying 150 homes and killing 60 people. Tsunami are not caused by the moon's course but by earthquake tremors or shifts in the sea bed many miles offshore. They reach a maximum speed of 600 miles per hour. Today, advance warning systems give people time to reach higher ground.*

FRANCE

Beauvais
Paris

October 5, 1930
The crash of the R101

First officer of R101, Lieutenant Commander Atherstone, made an entry in his diary, the day before the R101 crash:

'Everybody is rather keyed up now, as we all feel that the future of airships very largely depends on what sort of show we put up. There are very many unknown factors and I feel that that thing called "Luck" will figure rather conspicuously in our flight. Let's hope for good luck and do our best . . .'

Amid cheers from a large crowd gathered in the fields below at 6.36 on October 4, 1930, the R101 left her mooring tower at Cardington, north of London, and set out on her maiden voyage for India. Aboard were the cream of aviation development engineering—men like Atherstone, Major G H Scott, Colonel Richmond, Wing Commander Colmore, and the Captain, Flight Lieutenant Irwin, one of the most senior and experienced airship flyers in the country. Some prominent civil service officials were also present, pleased at last to take part in this historic journey—Sir Sefton Brancker, Director of Civil Aviation at the Ministry, and Lord Thomson, Secretary of State for Air. Six officials from the Royal Airship Works and Lord Thomson's valet brought the total to 54 people. First stop was to be Ismailia,

The R101 rests at her mooring at Cardington, ready for her maiden voyage to India. With this flight the Air Ministry hoped to inaugurate a new Commonwealth transport service.

Suez Canal.

As the R101 moved steadily south, she sent out regular radio messages so that her course could be followed. She circled over Bedford, then rose to 1000 feet, then to 1500 feet as she moved towards London. As the airship left her mooring, she gave a slight lurch, so Irwin ordered water ballast to be dropped at once. A warning from the meteorological office had told him to expect winds of up to 40 to 50mph, worse than any conditions a British airship had experienced over land in the past.

As the ship passed over Hitchin, Hertfordshire, a housewife was horrified to see it so low in the air; it barely cleared the trees around her home. She could see into the airship quite clearly. There the distinguished passengers were enjoying a celebratory dinner, and the candelabra were gleaming on snow-white tablecloths.

At 8.21pm the airship reported, 'Over London. All well. Moderate rain . . . course now set for Paris.' The message also gave the wind speed as 25 miles an hour—less than anticipated. As the ship passed over the Channel, a moderately serious engine problem occurred, but by the time R101 reached the French Coast the engineers had corrected it. The winds picked up over the sea, and the airship slowly lost height, until it reached the alarmingly low level of about 750 feet. At 10pm, the height coxswain (whose sole responsibility was maintaining correct altitude) received a visit from Lt Commander Atherstone, who took over the wheel himself for a while until considerable increase in height had been achieved. Then he handed back the controls to the coxswain, warning him not to let the R101 go below 1000 feet again.

At 11pm the watch was changed, and the night crew came on duty. At midnight, the airship sent out a further message. In spite of the rough weather conditions and serious trouble in maintaining height, its words betrayed no real fears on the part of the airship's guests and crew:

'After an excellent supper our distinguished passengers smoked a final cigar and having sighted the French coast have now gone to bed to rest after the excitement of their leave-taking. All essential services are functioning satisfactorily. The crew have settled down to watch-keeping routine.'

R101 sent out regular position reports at 1.28 and at 1.51, by which time she was approaching Beauvais, north of Paris. As she passed slightly to east of the town, many people heard the drone of her engines, and those who had been awaiting the sound rushed to the windows to catch a glimpse of this historic sight: the vast silver-white cigar-shaped dirigible floating over their heads with its warning lights twinkling, buffeted by rain and storm clouds.

Just outside Beauvais, with no warning at all, the R101 went into a steep dive. It tilted so sharply that the engineers manning the ship were thrown off-balance, and furniture shot forward

across the decks. The height coxswain pulled hard on his wheel in an effort to right the ship and got the airship once more to its proper height. But within seconds the ship lunged downwards again and this time the cox could do nothing to pull her out of the dive.

The officers in command could see what was coming. They ordered all engines to be cut dead, although only one was stopped, and warning bells were rung. It is difficult to imagine, but there was no panic. Airship flight is normally so smooth and buoyant and altitude changes so much a part of the pattern, that few people would leap to the idea of 'crashing' in the way that modern aircraft might. The chief coxswain had time to go aft, where the crew were sleeping, to announce quite matter-of-factly, 'We're down, lads.'

With a great grinding noise of engines ceasing and metal grating on metal, the airship lumbered to the earth and slid several yards along the ground. Then it burst into flames: the bags of hydrogen, the gas that kept it afloat, roared up instantaneously on ignition. Only one man actually saw the R101 catch fire—Eugene Rabouille, a local factory worker out hunting rabbits, described the last moments of this great enterprise:

'I clearly saw the passengers' quarters, well-lit, and the green and red lights on the right and left of the airship. Suddenly there was a violent squall. The airship dipped by the nose several times, and its forepart crashed into the northwest edge of the Bois des Coutumes. There was at once a tremendous explosion, which knocked me down.

'Soon flames rose into the sky to a great height—perhaps 300 feet. Everything was enveloped by them. I saw human figures running about like madmen in the wreck. Then I lost my head and ran away into the woods.'

The sight of the helpless dying is not one to attract a man caught by surprise: of the 54 people on board, seven escaped. They were extremely lucky. Most of the survivors were in the engine car, where one of the water ballast tanks burst, inundating it. This protected the six men there from the intense heat of the surrounding fire and

Left The interior structure of the R101, showing the massive steel frame required to support the 17 gasbags that gave the airship its lift. *Above* A sample of the elegant fittings inside the R101. On her maiden voyage the airship was carrying the top men of British aviation.

gave them a few seconds' grace. They jumped through a small opening, the port quarter on the lefthand side of the stern. Harry Leech, the only official from the Royal Airship Works who survived, got away by hacking a hole in the passengers' 'smoking room' and literally jumping through the burning body of the ship. He landed in the branches of a tree, and as it was raining, the leaves showered water all over him. In his own laconic words, this 'cooled me off'.

Next day, nothing remained of the glorious R101 but a massive tangle of scorched metal. What bodies could be found were brought back to London for a memorial service at St Paul's Cathedral and a requiem mass at Westminster Cathedral before removal to their final resting place, a communal grave at Cardington. Later, a memorial was built at the site of the crash at Beauvais.

What caused the destruction of the R101, and the appalling loss of so many adventurous and talented men? The R101 was built of dreams, and with its end, British airship hopes vanished.

Airships had been pioneered by the German inventor Count Von Zeppelin. Together with Dr Hugo Eckener, he set up the Zeppelin Company, which between 1910–14 made more than 2000 flights carrying 10,000 or more passengers in their first four ships, the *Schwaben*, *Viktoria Luise*, *Hansa* and *Sachsen*. Most of these flights were local, not more than about two hours long.

The basis of airship construction is simple. Large balloons containing lighter-than-air gas, either hydrogen or helium, were strapped around a metal inner structure where the cabins, decks and engine rooms were housed. Around the whole, a large cigar-shaped outer skin was pulled tightly into place. The gasbags provided the lift; engines provided the forward motion. Large bags of water ballast were added so height could be regulated by dropping weight as the ship rose. As it climbed higher scoops on the outside envelope collected rainwater or condensation from wet clouds, so that water-weight could be renewed during the flight. The emergency ballast bags were shaped like trousers, called 'lederhosen' by the Zeppelin crews. If the ship came down too low during a flight, the height coxswain pulled a lever on his control panel. The water bags could be emptied in a matter of seconds, as the R101 had done almost immediately after take-off.

The first British models were close copies of the Zeppelins. A German airship, the L33, was captured in 1916 when it made a forced landing in Essex. From it, the British evolved the R33, R34 and R38. In 1919 the R34 made a successful return journey across the Atlantic, and the R33 completed a total of 800 hours' flying without mishap. The R38 was less fortunate. On August 24, 1921, it broke in two while maneouvring in mid-air, travelling at its maximum speed of 60 miles an hour, and plummeted into the Humber River. Forty-four lives were lost. The fault appeared to lie in R38's construction. No allowances had been made for the stresses and strains

set up by steering the airship at high speeds. A great deal still had to be learned about airship design and consruction.

It seems strange today that 60mph should be considered fast, but the outstanding feature of airships was their speed related to their enormous size. While small two-seater aircraft could zip along at several hundred miles an hour in the 'twenties, no one could conceive of jumbo jets. Heavier-than-air planes were seen as limited passenger carriers, whereas the great airships could accommodate 20 to 50 people at a time. Aeroplanes generally made short hops and did not do much night-flying. The airships could maintain a steady 60mph night and day and did not need to land often for refuelling. So even the R38 disaster did not stop imaginative minds from contemplating a great airship future.

The ultimate scheme came from Sir Samuel Hoare when he was Secretary of State for Air. He planned a transcontinental fleet of airships to link all the countries of the Commonwealth, to bind them together in a closer political and social union than had ever been contemplated. Airships would allow freer travel; news and ideas would spread swiftly, and trade would improve immeasurably, as airships had great potential as cargo carriers as well.

With this in mind, two airships were ordered in 1928: the R100 and the R101. The R100 was built as a private enterprise, inspired by the leading British supporter of lighter-than-air vehicles, Sir Dennistoun Burney. Its manufacture was in the hands of the Airship Guarantee Company, a subsidiary of Vickers. Reputedly to prevent this firm's getting a monopoly in the air as it had with submarine development, the Government decided to build the other ship, the R101, under its own authority and set up a 'rival' concern at Cardington—the Royal Airship Works.

Almost at once, disparities appeared between the two organizations. R100 had the best designer in the country, B N Wallis, who was later responsible for the Wellington bomber and the dambuster bomb. The government project at Cardington had at its head Lt-Colonel Vincent Richmond. He had considerable experience with balloons and with German airship technique, but less practical knowledge than Wallis. At a personal level, however, the two teams had close, if competitive, relationships.

Sir Samuel Hoare organized the building of various mooring towers to link up his projected Commonwealth service. The earliest were erected at Ismailia in Egypt, Karachi, India and Montreal, Canada. Each mast was a major task, higher than Nelson's column and fitted with a lift, searchlights, spiral staircase and winches to pull the ships into position. There were underground fuel tanks holding 10,000 gallons of diesel oil, with a pump capable of raising the fuel to a height of 400 feet. Other pumps were installed to supply 5000 gallons of water an hour. Each tower, 200 feet high and 70 feet across at the base, could withstand a pull of 30 tons in any direction at the top and cost £50,000 to build.

However, the government project at Cardington, paid for by public money, always had to cut corners. Although steel was used for the frame instead of duralumin, which had been used in the R38, the same problematic fabric was used for the gasbags. In these days of synthetic materials in seemingly endless varieties, it is difficult to imagine the difficulties and limitations faced by the R101 team. For their gasbags they used 'gold-beaters skin', made from the membrane of bullock's intestines laboriously stitched together. The skins were imported from the Chicago cattle market, and it is estimated that more than a million animals supplied the fabric for the R101 bags.

Hundreds of wires held the 17 gasbags in position around the frame. During test runs, the bags seemed to chafe against the metal structure, so 4000 special cushions were added to prevent any further damage to them. New valves were especially designed so the amount of gas in the bags could be carefully controlled. Unfortunately, they were so sensitive that an unexpected roll or lurch in the airship would make them release gas. The ship could easily lose height at a time when it did not intend to.

All these relatively minor problems were the kind of design-and-development headache that might be anticipated with any ambitious project. Given time, most of them would be corrected.

But the R101 had no time. In 1929 when the Government changed, Lord Thomson became Secretary of State for Air. He too was an airship enthusiast, and he decided on a magnificent launching trip for the government's project at Cardington. He would fly in the R101 to India himself in the autumn of 1930.

Thomson has been subsequently blamed by many experts for putting pressure on the R101 team. He felt that in a public venture, there should be some demonstration of confidence and success before too much money and time had been spent. He maintained before the flight that he deferred to the experts' opinion on progress and would never countermand their wishes nor

Above left *The R101 in action. The airship threw out water ballast as she rose from the mooring tower.*
Below left *French officials examine the twisted metal wreckage of the airship where she crashed, just north of Paris at Beauvais. There were only seven survivors out of the 54 men on board.*

put public relations before individual safety.

On the other hand, the R101 team came under a great deal of pressure from the success of their rivals, the R100 team. That ship had been launched in December 1929. Although she proved heavy (about seven tons over), she was very manouverable and a fast flyer, reaching 80mph top speed. On July 29 the following year, the R100 left on a round trip to Canada and back. Though the outer covering fabric was ripped twice during storms, the ship's general performance was admirable. The R100 tried diesel engines, like the R101, in the early stages, but gave them up and went back to Rolls Royce Condor aero-engines. These weighed nine tons in comparison with the R101's seventeen, although the R100 had to carry correspondingly more fuel to cover the same distance.

There is no doubt that the success of the R100 added steam to the R101 efforts at Cardington, where the whole team was anxious to prove that their airship was as good, if not better. Her first flight had been made in October 1929, but her major public showing took place during the Royal Air Force Display at Hendon on June 28, 1930. The great airship flew low over the heads of the crowd at about 500 feet. Little did the excited airship enthusiasts watching realize that the R101 had in fact gone into a steep dive, only pulled out by swift, skilful handling by the coxswain.

The ship was flying 'heavy': something had to be done before the well-publicized trip to India could take place on schedule three months later. It was decided to split the ship in two and add an extra bay, to give greater volume. The ship's diameter at its maximum was 132 feet; its capacity 5,508,800 cubic feet; its gross lift 167·2 tons. R100 kept to its original size, 144,400 cubic metres. After the disaster, this difference led to heated argument over the wisdom of increasing R101's length.

In those final hectic months, the ship was not only stretched but a whole new outer skin was sewn in place. The airship was ready on September 25. Foul weather looked as if it would postpone the final test flights until October, but the skies cleared enough on September 30 for a last-minute trial run.

Immense debate has centred on the thoroughness of the final tests. It is held by some experts that vital reports on the R101's airworthiness were not complete when the Air Ministry issued the appropriate Certificate on October 2, without which the flight to India could not take place. The verdict of the Court of Inquiry on this point was: 'The R101 started for India before she could be regarded as having emerged successfully from all the exhaustive steps proper to the experimental stage.'

It is extraordinary that after all the efforts to lighten the ship by lengthening it and jettisoning some non-vital mechanical devices, the R101 set off on her first official voyage bulging with bric-a-brac. Pale blue Axminster carpeting was laid in the passengers' quarters; silver dining sets and cutlery were put aboard. Elegant potted palms dotted the bamboo-furnished lounge and smoking room. The luxury of the fitments can hardly be imagined in the modern age of streamlined plastic jet-travel. To compensate for additional weight, the crew had left their parachutes behind. How could wool carpeting remain?

Publicity was partly to blame, for at the Imperial conference in London in November 1929, when the airship service had been announced, one reporter proudly claimed: 'The R101 will provide luxuries undreamed of by Jules Verne and H G Wells. It will positively be an aerial hotel.'

General conclusions on the cause of the R101 disaster centre around its weight, although the exact finding of the Court of Enquiry, published on April 1, 1931, was that the airship came down with a sudden loss of gas in a forward gasbag at a time when the nose of the craft was being depressed by a downward current of air.

'In the construction of the R101 the designers broke away almost completely from conventional methods . . . originality and courage in design are not to be deprecated, but there is an obvious danger in giving too many separate hostages to fortune at one time.'

So much faith and confidence had been placed in the R100 and R101 that at first newsmen on night duty refused to believe the reports of the Beauvais crash. Only the *Express* ran the story in their Sunday edition. The shock of the disaster was so great that it put a stop to further airship development in the UK. The R100 (ironically the more successful in design and performance) was kept on the ground for a year, finally broken up and sold for scrap at £400. Worse still, so many talented men died in R101 that the development of civil aviation in Great Britain was set back years. No comparable disaster has hit any industry in quite the same way, before or after R101.

There can be no doubt that political necessities behind the R101 affected its development. Harry Leech, the survivor who landed in a tree, went to work for Sir Malcolm and Donald Campbell later in their efforts to break water and land speed records. He commented, 'One thing R101 proved is that politics and experimental work don't mix.' Another conclusion is that the R101 project was too fraught, too ambitious. Dr Hugo Eckener, the great Zeppelin expert, was once shown the plans for the R101. 'Very nice', he said, 'but isn't it a little big?' The final word of judgement came from the Court of Enquiry:

'It is impossible to avoid the conclusion that the R101 would not have started for India on the evening of the 4th October if it had not been that reasons of public policy were considered as making it highly desirable for her to do so if she could.'

In spite of Lord Thomson's protests, political expediency was to blame.

Right The smoking stern of the Morro Castle *lies beached at Asbury Park, New Jersey. On the quayside stands a fascinated crowd of local residents.*

September 8, 1934
Fire on the Morro Castle

Above One of the Morro
Castle's *lifeboats is washed
on to the shore by waves at
Spring Lake, New Jersey.
Because the sea was calm
and the water warm, some
survivors swam ashore.

There are few stories of sea disasters that can
match that of the *Morro Castle* for mystery and
sheer human stupidity. Error upon error resulted
in the total destruction of the 11,520-ton vessel
and the loss of 134 lives.

September 7, 1934: the Ward Line cruiser
Morro Castle was speeding along the east coast of
the USA, bound for New York. It was near the
end of a successful trip to Havana, and passengers
were busily exchanging addresses and packing
their souvenirs.

Last-night celebrations were marred by the
sudden illness of the Captain. Late in the evening
he had complained of stomach pains and within
an hour was found dead in his cabin. Captain
Robert Willmott was only 55. The senior ship's
surgeon, Dr De Witt Van Zile, could only find
'acute indigestion' as the cause of death.

Willmott's close friend and chief officer,
William Warms, assumed command of the ship.
His first duty was to send a message to the Ward
Line offices, informing his employers of the
Captain's death. Then he checked the ship's
course. The *Morro Castle* was approaching New
Jersey, her powerful turbo-electric engines
pounding through stormy seas. The *Scotland
Lightship* and the New York channel lay ahead.
The liner was keeping to her time schedule and
proceeding normally.

Below, however, things were far from calm. A
small fire had broken out in the passengers'
library and writing room. At first three sailors
tried to cope with the blaze themselves. (Almost
exactly 30 years later a similar fire broke out on
the *Lakonia*, and the same stupid mistake was
made—crew tried to put out the blaze by themselves before warning the captain officially. In
both cases, precious fire-fighting time was lost.)
In the case of the *Morro Castle*, the incident was
not an isolated one. A fire in her hold on a previous trip had been blamed on Cuban communist
agitators or some criminal element of New York's
rough waterfront population.

The sailors found they could not control the
fire. Before long, curls of smoke were creeping
silently along the deck corridors. The ship's
owners had made great publicity of the *Morro
Castle*'s modern fire-proofing systems, yet no
general alarm sounded, and the crew were totally
unable to check the fire's spread.

The chief radio operator George Rogers was
summoned from his bunk by his assistant George
Alagna. Realizing the fire was spreading, Rogers
went to his post at the radio and sent Alagna to the
bridge to see what instructions he could get from
the acting captain, Warms. Minutes ticked by and
no news came back. Rogers dispatched his second
assistant Maki with the same message: 'Find out
what signals they want me to send'.

By now, smoke was billowing along all the corridors, yet no word came from the bridge. Warms
must have assumed that his crew would even-

tually gain control of the fire. Perhaps his thoughts were wandering with the Captain's death weighing on his mind. Whatever led to his lack of decision, the *Morro Castle* continued on her course at full speed, 21 knots, with the disastrous effect of fanning the fire like a huge natural bellows. Soon all the deck structures were lapped with tongues of flame.

The time was now about 3am. Awakened by the smell of burning, passengers began to mill about the decks and corridors. There was no official announcement, and no message was sent out via the crew to get the passengers into the lifeboats.

At 3.13 Rogers heard a message on his radio. A nearby ship, the *Andrea Luckenbach*, was calling the shore station and asking if there was news of a ship on fire nearby—they could see smoke rising above the waves. Rogers, having no instructions about sending any definite message, could only tap out a 'stand by' signal, 'CQ' which he repeated three times. Once again he sent Alagna, his assistant, for orders from the bridge. Alagna was impatient with running about and was getting desperate. He did not think anyone on the bridge could give a satisfactory answer, and by now most crew and passengers were concerned only with escape.

The *Andrea Luckenbach*, the *Monarch of Bermuda*, the *President Cleveland*, the *City of Savannah*, the coastguard cutter *Tampa* and a navy destroyer, USS *Chester*, converged on the *Morro Castle* in answer to Roger's messages. Now passengers began to jump overboard to save themselves from the blaze. Launching the lifeboats was chaotic and slow. People got so desperate that they preferred to trust themselves to the mercy of the waves than stand about choking in the smoke and heat of the rapidly burning decks. One crewman from New York, Leroy C Kelsey, described the scene:

'Black smoke poured down stairways and there was a rush of running feet. Flames cracked and roared and the black windows were shot with red and yellow gleams—were there people in there? We were trapped on the port side of the dying ship; three girls, too young to die, myself and several men in the uniform of the steward's department.'

Whole families went overboard together, like the Phelps—a New York doctor, his wife and 25-year-old son. Two sisters, Gladys and Ethel Knight, went over the side, Ethel clutching a small 7-year-old boy, Benito Rueda of Brooklyn. Luckily the water was warm, and the waves helped to push people in towards the New Jersey shore.

At last, at 3.20, Warms gave the signal for Rogers to send the SOS message, now hopelessly overdue. A few lifeboats were lowered on the starboard side. On the port side, flames were too

Above *The ocean liner remained stranded at Asbury Park for several months. Eager tourists paid for admission tickets to get a close look at what was left of 'The pride of the Havana run'.*

Overleaf *The cause of the* Morro Castle *blaze remains a mystery. The official enquiry could only state it as 'spontaneous combustion'.*

intense for anyone to get near. Rogers continued at his post, sending out details of position, '20 miles south of Scotland Light'. His last message: 'Hurry, can't hold out much longer', came just before the generator exploded in the heat.

Alagna got hold of Rogers, by now in a semi-collapsed state, and together they stumbled along the decks and corridors to the bridge. Eight lifeboats got away; only 15 people including Warms and Rogers remained on board the blazing liner. About 4am, the *Andrea Luckenbach* neared the scene of the disaster and picked up 11 persons flailing about in the open sea. Then the *President Cleveland* arrived. It launched two lifeboats and searched for one and a half hours but found no survivors. The *City of Savannah* picked up one, Margaret Cotter of Springfield, Massachusetts, who had kept afloat for five hours. A coastguard boat from New Jersey gathered 70 souls and ferried between the ocean and the *Luckenbach* with its load, searching again and again for more.

Some people actually managed to reach the shore unaided, crawling exhausted on to the beach at Sea Girt. Local residents, watching the smoke billows of the flaming *Morro Castle*, ran forward to help them. The two sisters, Gladys and Ethel Knight (still clutching Benito) were nearly ashore when they were rescued by small boats.

As usually happens after a disaster, crowds flocked to the scene to watch the end of the *Morro Castle*. This was one of the first tragedies to involve extensive 'action' news coverage. Scores of light planes hovered over the burning wreck transmitting live reports for radio and newspapers, helping to swell the crowd at Asbury Park, the New Jersey town near where the *Morro Castle* lay floundering in the rough ocean.

Of the 318 passengers, 90 died; of the 231 crew, 44. Some reports claimed that the crew behaved badly, saving their own skins and neglecting their duty to assist the rest. But the main blame must lie with the officers who apparently did nothing to command obedience or create disciplined escape procedures and quell panic. The evidence of the lifeboats is damning. One was lowered with 13 aboard, another with three. The capacity of each was 70. Only eight lifeboats with 85 persons in them were pulled ashore.

The coastguard cutter *Tampa* attempted a salvage operation of the *Morro Castle*. All day Saturday, September 8, crowds watched in fascination as the cutter laboured to tow the hulk past Sea Girt and up to New York harbour. As senior coastguard officer, Captain Earl Rose had power to order Warms, the acting captain, and the few remaining crew, including radio man Rogers, to leave the ship. There was not much left of the *Morro Castle*. A reporter from the London *Daily Express* filed this graphic description viewed from an aeroplane circling above the wreck:

'. . . Flaming patches of oil floated on the surface of the sea. Great clouds of steam went up

from the water's edge . . . All the superstructure was burnt. The funnels just melted away in the intense heat.'

The *Tampa* had to give up the struggle to tow the *Morro Castle* to a safe mooring: the sea had roughened again and the weight of the liner was slowly pulling the cutter towards the beach. The towline finally broke and (to the delight of the sightseers) the *Morro Castle* fell away into the surging waves and came to rest on the shore at Asbury Park. It remained a tourist attraction for months, with visitors buying tickets to come and stare at what had once been 'The pride of the Havana run'. It was finally towed to Baltimore for scrap in March 1935.

The enquiry put the cause as 'spontaneous combustion'. No one established how the fire started, although it may have been caused by the ship's funnel which passed very close behind the library wall near the start of the fire, overheating the wood panelling of the room. A federal court found Chief Officer Warms and Chief Engineer Abbot guilty of misconduct, negligence and failure to their duty, but they were spared prison sentences on appeal.

A bizarre story surrounds the radio officer George Rogers. He was considered a hero for sticking to his post and contacting other vessels in spite of a lack of clear orders from the bridge. He joined a New Jersey police force, but was later convicted of planting a bomb with intent to injure his superior officer. After 11 years, he was back in prison, this time on a charge of murder, for which he received a life sentence. He had a criminal record dating back to the age of 12.

An American author, Thomas Gallagher, wrote a dramatic reconstruction of the *Morro Castle* disaster, published shortly after Rogers died in 1958. Gallagher tried to show that Rogers murdered the Captain and set fire to the ship deliberately. There is little beyond flimsy circumstantial evidence and Rogers' criminal background to support the theory. The ship's doctor, who died in the flames, could not even be questioned on the exact cause of the Captain's death.

The enquiry found two clear explanations for the rapid spread of the fire. First, the ship, designed as it was for cruises in warm tropical seas, had an open-deck construction that allowed the flames to spread easily from deck to deck. Also, Warms had allowed the liner to continue her course at between 18 and 20 knots in a high wind, with the obvious effect of whipping up the flames even more.

The *Morro Castle* disaster continued to affect people's lives long after the event. Chief Officer Warms went back to sea as second officer on another ship, the *Cauto*, which foundered in the Gulf of Mexico. He never eluded the taint of catastrophe that seemed to haunt him. Ethel Knight, who had saved 7-year-old Benito Rueda, married soon after, but died of a heart attack four weeks later. The Massachusetts Humane Society awarded her a silver medal, posthumously.

Right *A coastguard acting commander returns to shore with another victim of the fire. Of 318 passengers, 90 died; of 231 crew, 44 were lost.*

50

May 6, 1937
The burning of the Hindenburg

The Hindenburg was a landmark in passenger transport; the culmination of a lifetime's work for two airship experts of world renown, Dr Hugo Eckener and Count von Zeppelin. She was the largest and most elegant lighter-than-air craft ever designed. 814 feet long with a maximum diameter of 135 feet, she cruised at a steady 80 knots, driven by four 100-horsepower Daimler diesel engines. Inside her frame a total of 14 miles of metal bracing supported her, with buoyancy supplied from 16 gasbags filled with hydrogen.

On her lower deck, the crew accommodation, the kitchens, the officers' dining-room, bars, showers and a ballroom were built along the centre spine of the ship. Above, on the 'A' deck were 25 splendid state-rooms, fitted with luxurious carpeting, drapes and bed covers, with wash-basins, wardrobes and mirrors. On the port side of the top deck was the passengers' dining-room and promenade; on the starboard side a lounge with a grand piano. A reading and writing room and another promenade completed the interior.

Launched on March 4, 1936, the Hindenburg soon passed all her test runs and successfully completed her maiden voyage to South America. In that year she made seven voyages to Brazil and ten to the USA, mooring at Lakehurst, New Jersey, south of New York. To travel her was the height of style, and the transatlantic fare was so enormous that only high society and the world's self-made men could even contemplate the trip. Even so, there was a long waiting list of would-be passengers. So great was the German Zeppelin Company's confidence in the Hindenburg that in the winter of 1936, the airship was temporarily removed from service to be refitted to take even more passengers. Eleven extra cabins were added, bringing the maximum passenger capacity to 72.

Dr Hugo Eckener, the ship's designer, was unhappy about one of the Hindenburg's first duties after the alterations were completed. Goebbels, the Nazi propaganda chief, had insisted that the airship be used for a trip around Germany carrying leading military figures and Nazi party officials. There was some rush in servicing the Hindenburg, and she experienced engine troubles

on her next trip, the regular flight to Rio de Janeiro at the end of March.

However, these problems were soon corrected and the Hindenburg was declared fit. She was booked to capacity for the first flight of the year to Lakehurst. On the evening of May 3, 1937, she left on the first of 18 scheduled voyages for the year. The sea-crossing took only 16 hours—surprisingly fast, even from the standpoint of present-day air transport.

At Lakehurst Naval Air Station where the Hindenburg was expected to arrive at about 8am on May 6, 1937, the usual crowd of staff reporters, newsreel cameramen and radio interviewers gathered in leisurely fashion. The arrival of the Hindenburg was so routine that it simply received 'society' coverage when a well-known figure was aboard. Consequently, the facilities for news coverage at Lakehurst were rudimentary,

with just one telephone set aside for the pressmen's use.

The crowd of relatives and sightseers were getting a little impatient. German efficiency for once was thwarted, because the airship was late. Captain Max Pruss had sent a radio message in the afternoon announcing his intention to circle for a while as he could see storm clouds brewing up. It rained quite hard about 4pm, but by early evening the weather improved slightly, with only a light drizzle and mild wind blowing. The landing crew, consisting of 110 navy men and 138 civilians, bustled around the mooring mast and customs facilities, expecting the airship to cruise over at any moment.

Around 7pm the Hindenburg glided in towards her berth at the mooring mast. She was a truly amazing sight, a great shining silver-grey object, shaped like a bomb, with steerage fins sloping up at the rear, top and bottom.

At 7.19 the Captain gave the order for the water ballast to be dropped, and for the gasbag valves to be closed. The Hindenburg dropped to about 200 feet, hanging in the wind and slowly edging up to the mooring mast. Then the engines were reversed to prevent the airship overshooting her mark or moving in too fast. The whole operation was proceeding in the routine clock-work manner that had created the great Zeppelin reputation. At 7.21 the landing ropes were lowered and some of the ground crew set about hauling them in. Then the steel mooring cable appeared from the nose of the ship, and more crewmen looked up expectantly, ready to winch the ship to her resting place.

One reporter, Herb Rau of the *Standard News*, had already turned his back on the airship, heading towards the one telephone so that he could be first to get in his story that the Hindenburg had arrived safely.

The passengers were clearly visible to the people standing below. The ship was only 75 feet above the ground. Relatives were waving at the faces peering out of the promenade deck windows, when suddenly they saw an awe-inspiring flash of fire burst out on the top of the ship. Mouths went dry. The Hindenburg, the safest airship in the world, was going up in flames.

One of the most historic moments in aeronautical history was captured for all the world to see and hear by that crowd of news reporters standing below. Herbert Morrison, an announcer with Station WLS, Chicago, was blithely filling his listeners in when suddenly his tone changed to near-hysteria. 'Its broken into flames. It's flashing—flashing! It's flashing terribly! It's bursting into flames and falling on the mooring mast!'

Below left The Hindenburg cruises over Manhattan on her last flight.

Below right The stern sinks to the ground, ablaze. The Captain's quick thinking allowed a few people to escape.

Someone shouted 'Run!' and the ground crew, the families, friends and reporters began an almost machine-like movement to get out of the way. This must have been the moment of truth for the Hindenburg's passengers, for inside the airship, most people had only felt a slight thud and passed it off as part of the mooring manoeuvres. Even Captain Pruss had no knowledge of the fire at this stage. A mechanic, George Haupt, saw the fire in gas cell number 4 in the stern of the ship: he gave the alarm and Pruss was contacted by the radio officer who gave him the news.

It was good timing, for when the Hindenburg began to slide out of level, Captain Pruss made a decision that gave a chance of survival to a few passengers and crew. Instead of pulling the blazing airship up to horizontal, he let the stern sink to the ground so some people could jump out.

Bodies were thrown about like beads in a box. Horrified eye witnesses saw small figures, outlined black against the orange glare of the spreading fire, plummeting to the ground. Herbert Morrison was still shouting into his microphone: 'This is terrible! This is one of the worst catastrophes in the world. Oh the humanity and all the passengers! I told you, it's a mass of smoking wreckage, Honest, I can hardly breathe'. He had to stop, as the scene was too shocking for him to be able to continue.

The flames spread first towards the stern, as this part fell to the earth, then leaped along the length of the airship to the front, sticking high up in the air, outlined in a lurid glow. In a matter of moments the whole ship was a mass of flames, and the great Hindenburg crashed to the ground.

Some newsreelmen stood gaping, so shocked that they held their cameras pointing at the ground for quite some time before they came to their professional senses and grabbed at equipment to start filming. One photographer, Murray Becker of Associated Press, was among the few who managed to function and made an historic collection of pictures, the first to reach New York. He described the scene as 'a moment of spectacular madness'. Later in the night, when the disaster was over, he collapsed and cried, looking at the wreck.

Less than half the people inside the Hindenburg survived. Its structure, with 600,000 square feet of fabric and its highly inflammable gasbags meant that the airship was totally destroyed in just over half a minute. Some passengers on the promenade deck smashed windows and hurled themselves out as the airship slid to the earth. Many who managed to get out were crushed by falling metal or burned by the flames before they could clear the wreckage. As the ship fell, it gave a bounce, shooting up again to 100 feet. Some people on the port side mistimed their jumps and fell to their deaths before the ship came down to a safer height once more. One man who dropped on to the wet sand of the landing area escaped the burning wreckage by virtually tunnelling a channel through the ground. Others trying to scramble out of the way found their feet sinking, sucked into the wet surface. A few, with no recollection of how they got out, may simply have been blown clear by the explosion.

Among the last to think of escape were the veteran officers of the Hindenburg: Captain Pruss, Ernst Lehmann (who had taken the Hindenburg on her maiden voyage to South America) and six other senior crewmen. They got out only when the airship came to her final rest on the ground. Max Pruss even then refused to get clear but ran around the burning wreck trying to find passengers and help them to escape. Eventually he had to be physically restrained by three American sailors and was led away, still protesting, with the entire back of his uniform burned away.

The final number of dead was 36: 22 crew, 13 passengers, and one ground crew who failed to run clear of the falling ship. Those who survived were given immediate medical attention by nurses and doctors summoned to Lakehurst by the radio coverage of the event. Most on-the-spot treatment consisted of first aid for burns, some of appalling severity, and administration of morphine to deaden the pain. But many people were so deeply shocked that they felt nothing, even in the most frightful condition. One or two people were able to talk quite calmly and rationally for a few moments, as if safe and fit, before death overtook them, so bad were their burns. After first aid treatment, the injured were taken to hospitals in the vicinity.

Among those who clearly would not live long was the senior Captain of the Zeppelin, Ernst Lehmann. An immediate concern of the officials at Lakehurst was to establish the cause of the accident, and it was therefore vital that Lehmann and any other experienced crew member should reveal what they could about the moments before the fire. The commandant of the Lakehurst station, Charles Rosendahl, put a guard watch on the wreck, so that it could be properly investigated without any clues being disturbed or looted. Then he went to visit Lehmann. The only suggestion that the ex-captain could make was 'lightning'; he could give no other explanation for the airship's sudden destruction.

Dr Hugo Eckener, head of the Zeppelin Company, had other ideas. He got the news in the middle of the night when a reporter from the New York Times rang to tell him the whole story. His first reaction was 'sabotage' but when he made this view public he was forced by his own government to retract it. At the time it would have been awkward politically for the Nazi government to be somehow involved in this major international disaster.

It was not the first time that Eckener had had difficulties with the Nazis. At the start, he had tactfully suggested that his new airship might be named after Adolph Hitler But the deeply superstitious Führer refused the honour, not wishing to have his name linked with anything that might go badly. If the airship were to crash, said Hitler, it would appear to all the world as a bad omen.

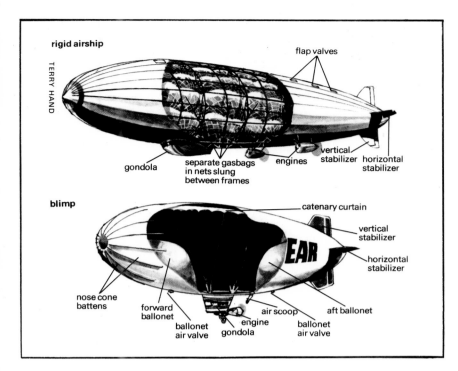

rigid airship

TERRY HAND

flap valves

gondola

separate gasbags in nets slung between frames

engines

vertical stabilizer

horizontal stabilizer

blimp

catenary curtain

vertical stabilizer

EAR

horizontal stabilizer

nose cone battens

forward ballonet

ballonet air valve

air scoop

engine gondola

aft ballonet

ballonet air valve

Above *Comparison of a rigid airship and a blimp. The ship has a steel frame and usually carries hydrogen-filled bags; the blimp is filled with helium and uses air compression to bring it back down to land.*

Instead, the new transatlantic airship was named after one of Germany's leading statesmen, President Paul von Hindenburg, who had died on August 2, 1934.

Forced to abandon the theory of sabotage, the experts, including Eckener, had to fall back on the 'lightning' suggestion. There was testimony at the official enquiry from members of the crew, that fire was clearly seen inside the craft before she went up in flames. But the enquiry overcame the conflicting evidence and concluded that hydrogen had leaked from one of the gasbags and, mixed with air, had ignited, probably due to electrical 'brush' discharge, commonly called 'St Elmo's fire'.

Hugo Eckener later gave support to this finding. Some of the crew had given evidence at the enquiry that the ship was handling 'stern-heavy' at the time, suggesting that a gasbag in the stern had indeed sprung a leak. 'Escaping gas would rise and fill the space inside the upper fin and beneath the outer cover', he wrote later. 'It would be set afire by an electrical discharge and at first would burn slowly until the fire reached the spot where the gas, streaming upwards, was being mixed with air to form an explosive mixture. This would produce an oxyhydrogen explosion which would instantly set fire to the gas within the damaged cell.'

Not everyone in Germany was happy with the scientific explanation. Anger was aroused by the recollection that the airship company had originally wanted helium, a light but less dangerous gas than hydrogen, for the buoyancy gasbags. But helium could only be acquired from the USA, who were reluctant to supply it to the Germans with the Nazi party growing daily more war-minded. Finally in March 1938, the American Secretary of the Interior forbade further export of helium, effectively ending hope of further air-

ship development by the Germans.

Captain Max Pruss survived his terrible injuries and returned to Germany to campaign for the continuance of airship design and building. But the Hindenburg had been too big a disaster, too exposed to the gaze of the world, and besides the Nazis were more interested in heavier-than-air development—for their fighter planes.

Pruss argued persistently with Göering, head of aviation and creator of the Luftwaffe. But the latter got his way. That other highly successful airship, the Graf Zeppelin (both the old and the new model of the same name), were reduced to scrap—probably for Luftwaffe planes.

The destruction of the Hindenburg signalled the end of the airship era. Never again were they used for long-distance passenger travel. While the R101 had been a major setback to British development, the Hindenburg struck the final note on a world-wide basis, largely due to the massive and immediate news coverage of the event.

Herbert Morrison recovered himself sufficiently to continue his running commentary of the disaster, interviewing those survivors who spoke English during the hectic evening hours that followed the crash. By 12 o'clock next day news theatres in New York were playing the newsreel film of the Hindenburg to packed houses—often accompanied by screaming and fainting in the audience. At 4.30 that afternoon, NBC repeated Herbert Morrison's entire broadcast for the whole nation. On May 11, 10,000 people crowded the New York dockside at Pier 86 where 28 European victims were taken back home aboard the SS *Hamburg*, amidst a formal Nazi ceremony.

Ironically, airships were to prove most useful in World War II against the Germans. The Americans concentrated on smaller non-rigid models known as 'blimps' and built up 14 fleet squadrons which specialized in submarine patrol and convoy escort work. The blimps had a moderate speed and a low flight path, so they could scan the water for submarines and spot minefields in the distance. At the peak of operations they covered 3,000,000 square miles of the Atlantic, Pacific and Mediterranean oceans and escorted 89,000 surface vessels without losing one. They scored a particular success in the straits of Gibraltar where they hung in the air and set up a magnetic barrier, so German U-boats could be detected and destroyed. After losing three submarines in quick succession, the Germans gave up the passage. Although lighter-than-air craft had proved disastrous in the field of passenger transport, in war 87 per cent were in operational readiness at all times, a record level of efficiency and reliability among all kinds of military aircraft.

After World War II came the jet aeroplane and airships could not compete. But today a few new helium-filled ships are being built for a variety of purposes including carrying exceptionally heavy loads, such as rocket launch craft, for oceanographic research, mapping and surveying, and most recently for tourist trips and advertising.

November 28, 1942
The Cocoanut Grove fire

Below The burnt-out shell of the Cocoanut Grove, one of Boston's most popular nightclubs in the early 1940s. Over four hundred and fifty people died in the blaze.

The evening of November 28, 1942, was more than usually festive in Boston's night club district. Alongside the jostling soldiers and sailors on leave from the war fronts in Europe were a great crowd of out-of-towners drawn by a major football game between Boston and Holy Cross. The score, Holy Cross 55, Boston 12, was a big upset; perhaps there was more than average excitement in the post-game celebrations.

The Cocoanut Grove was one of Boston's brightest clubs. It had been open for 15 years, but the sudden increase in clientele, mostly soldiers on leave, had shot the club into publicity and popularity. It had two levels inside, the upper one holding a revolving stage on which the 'floorshow' took place. Downstairs was the newly-decorated 'Melody Lounge' with simulated leather lining on the walls, fancy artificial palm trees scattered among the tables, and swathes of bright coloured silk looped from the ceiling.

That night around 10pm, the club was jammed to capacity with between 800 to 1000 people. Bandleader Mickey Alpert was just striking up the 'Star Spangled Banner' to announce the beginning of the floor show. Backstage, performers were powdering their noses, straightening their seams and fluffing up their curls. Downstairs in the Melody Lounge, a customer decided to make things a little cosier in his corner of the bar and removed a light bulb from its socket. The barman sent over his young waiter, a high-school boy named Stephen Tomaszewski, to replace the light. Stephen had only been in the place three weekends, making extra money for his family. In fact, his employment was illegal; he was under-age for working at night. He climbed on a chair and lit a match to see what he was doing. After-wards he said he remembered putting it out. Pos-sibly he did but at that moment, a sudden spurt of flame shot across the bar from one of the decorative palm trees nearby.

In only a matter of seconds the Cocoanut Grove was a scene of total uproar and panic. Flames spread rapidly. Hungry tongues of fire licked at the palm leaves, the silk drapes and the plastic upholstery. The mock leather walls began to give off clouds of dense black smoke, stinging eyes and gagging throats. Pandemonium broke loose.

The only visible entrance was the revolving door at the front of the Melody Lounge six or seven feet wide. The front windows on either side were divided into small sections lined with metal. Only the tiniest person had a chance to get through. The doorway was soon jammed with screaming people. There was another exit from the Lounge, but nobody knew about it. Up some steps through an office, a side door led to Pied-mont Street, where the main entrance to the Cocoanut Grove stood. But inside, people could see only blank walls. At the back, the club faced on to Shawmut Avenue but there all the windows had been boarded up to block out the light. The Cocoanut Grove was a smoke-filled inferno trap-ping hundreds of terrified human beings.

As people ran for the door, they beat at their hair, their clothes, their faces, as flames fell from the tatters of silk overhead and set those below alight. Anyone heading for the door could be knocked flat or kicked aside in the great stampede. One man headed blindly towards the back of the club, facing Shawmut Avenue. Mr John Gill from Arlington grabbed his wife and used his free arm to ward off the surge of bodies about him.

'One moment I was moving towards that sound of glass, dragging Margaret with me. The next few seconds or minutes, I couldn't say which, are blanks in my memory. I don't remember that we were borne through that little door but we must have been. I don't know whether we were shoved through or whether we crawled.'

There *were* exit doors in the club. Four led to Piedmont Street, four to Shawmut Avenue, and one to Broadway along the side. But like Mr Gill, no one seemed to see any doors or other means of escape, except the few lucky ones, who got out more by accident than good judgement.

Panic inside the night club was of violent pro-portions. One naval officer who tried to keep calm among people rushing to the revolving door had the uniform ripped off his back. He was found later, slumped among the over-turned tables and

the broken glass, dead.

Some people were so terrified that they screwed themselves into the windows at the back on Shawmut Avenue, having torn off part of the boarding. They got caught on the glass. When rescuers arrived, several had to be cut loose with oxy-acetylene blow torches. Some died where they hung, half in, half out of the blazing building.

A group of the floorshow performers got out to safety due to the quick thinking of one of the chorus boys, Marshall Cook. They were just on the way down some stairs leading from their dressing rooms to the stage when they found their path blocked by a sheet of flame. Cook grabbed one of the girls and swiftly pushed everyone, 35 in all, back up the stairs and out on to the roof. (The building only had two storeys.) There, he found a ladder, which he and some of the other boys held so that the girls could climb down over the side to within a safe jumping distance of the ground.

Several other people rushed down to the base-ment, hoping to find another way out. As the crowd going down got bigger, someone yelled,

Top Victims from the fire are given immediate first aid by firemen and volunteers.
Bottom Bodies of the many people trapped inside are removed. Service men on leave were quick to answer the call for help.

'We can't get out this way.' So everyone struggled in the dark to turn and fight towards another exit. A few escaped by locking themselves into a refrigerator room. Some others found a window at the back of the basement, smashed the glass and crawled through.

The fire roared unchecked. Suddenly part of the floor of the Melody Lounge gave way and many people fell through to the basement. By now, flames and smoke were so intense that most people inside the building were dying of asphyxiation, not burns.

The firemen arrived within a few minutes of the first report at 10.15pm and had the blaze under control within an hour. But when they managed to get the revolving door down, a ghastly sight met their eyes. Bodies were piled up six deep behind it. A door next to the main one had a special 'panic lock' that was supposed to release with pressure, but it had been bolted shut. Of the 800 customers in the club when the fire broke out, 433 died inside in the flames, though many more were added to the list later that night and the following day when their burns proved too severe for treatment.

The firemen worked until 6 in the morning removing the dead and injured. Several volunteers came forward to help in the grim task. A passing motorist, Joseph L Lord, a Navy man and a former fireman, grabbed a tool from a nearby vehicle and smashed a window, through which he clambered and pushed out five women. They were caught in the arms of waiting firemen. Mr Lord was overcome with shock at one stage, but after treatment at a nearby hospital, returned to help remove 46 bodies.

Civil Defence workers were called in to help maintain order and give on-the-spot first aid. The Red Cross sent 500 people from Boston and New York with special drugs for burn treatment. So great were the numbers of casualties pouring into the city hospitals that blood plasma had to be released from the city's war-preparedness stores. When nurses arrived to supervize the removal of the injured, they found many wandering around dazedly, while others were completely hysterical. One nurse knocked down two uncontrollable survivors with jiu jitsu.

In the city's hospitals, the dead lined the corridors. No move could be made to identify and list casualties until well into the following day.

William Reilly, Boston's Fire Commissioner, made an on-the-spot assessment of the fire at 2am, once the firemen had it under control. The holocaust had resulted in large part from panic. If people had kept their heads, it could have been possible to control the blaze and get everyone out. Instead 484 people, half the number of patrons in the club, were believed dead, although a later report reduced the death total to 474.

Next day the Mayor of Boston recalled that he had repeatedly warned people about the possibilities of war disasters: 'At every opportunity I have been urging the people of this city to be calm and quiet, cool and collected, in the event of an emergency'. His pleas had gone unheeded.

Perhaps the war atmosphere contributed to the low resistance of that nightclub crowd to the onslaught of terror and panic. The city's civil defence organization had a sad and timely dress rehearsal for possible war events, such as air attacks, in the work of identifying the dead and controlling the crowds who gathered all night and next day around the Cocoanut Grove. At one stage in the night martial law had to be proclaimed in the Cocoanut Grove area.

But it soon emerged that the behaviour of the Cocoanut Grove customers was not by any means the sole explanation for the disaster. The City Commissioner for Buildings revealed that there were neither proper regulations covering the use of decorations in night clubs nor legal requirements about the installing of sprinkler systems and siting of emergency exits. Robert Moulton, head of the National Fire Protection Association, said that part of the blame must rest on 'the chaotic condition of Boston's building laws, incompetent enforcement, political influence and careless management'.

In the months that followed, recriminations spread as wildly as the fire itself had. An immediate inspection of all other night clubs in the city took place, and there was a quick and complete overhaul of the relevant laws. A detailed enquiry was set up and finalized its report in November 1943. It recorded the cause of the fire as 'unknown', but noted that the club had been 'overcrowded beyond capacity'. It concluded that loss of life would have been much lower if exits had been accessible and clearly marked.

A spate of charges were levelled against officials concerned, though few ended in prison sentences. City Building Commissioner Mooney was indicted for failure to enforce building regulations; Captain J Bucigross, a senior police officer, for failure to enforce the fire regulations, and various builders and decorators were accused of supplying substandard materials. One of the club operators, Barnett Welansky, was found guilty of recklessly operating the night club, failing to provide sufficient fire equipment and neglecting fire hazards. He was imprisoned for 12 to 15 years.

Welansky was an easily identifiable target. Bucigross was later acquitted, although the Suffolk County Grand Jury held that there had been 'shifting of responsibility and a tendency by various officials in different important departments to rely too much on their subordinates without exercising sufficient and proper check'.

That was the real source of the disaster, as it so often is with man-made ones. Situations are allowed to slide, to drift, to get out of hand, until a major mistake shows up a failure or corruption of an organization. This disaster may have been heightened in its seriousness by the almost abnormal reaction of the crowd, but in wartime, even greater care should have been exercised by those who had the morale-building entertainment, the comfort and the safety of the general public in their charge.

December 24, 1953
Train crash at Tangiwai

Tangiwai is a spot between Auckland and Wellington, New Zealand, where a railway bridge crosses over the Whangaehu River. Its name is Maori, 'Wailing Waters'—appropriate in the light of its history for disasters.

On Christmas Eve, 1953, the postmaster at a small nearby railway town, Cyril Ellis, thought the river looked dangerously high. Heavy rains had been falling for several days, but did not account for the turbulence of water he saw that evening. By some intuition he went to investigate the bridge, which by 10.21pm was already under water. Mr Ellis suddenly remembered the oncoming Main Trunk Express. As it approached Auckland it would be travelling at full speed, and with the force of the water rising as it appeared to be, the train would be in great danger. He began to run along the railway track, in the path of the advancing train, whose engine and lights were just visible in the distance. He waved frantically at the driver. He said afterwards, 'I am sure the driver and fireman saw my signals but they just did not have enough distance in which to stop the train'. With an appalling screech of metal on metal, the train began to slide over the bridge. When it was halfway across, the railway bridge gave way under the weight of the water flooding down the Whangaehu, and the engine, moving at

Below The tangled remains of the Auckland express lie in the bed of the Whangaehu River. The railway bridge was washed away by flood water.

a speed of about 40 to 50mph, careered over the side of the destroyed bridge, taking with it the tender and the first five carriages. The sixth carriage rocked and hovered on the brink, the rest remained on the bank.

There was a rush among the passengers in the sixth compartment to clamber back to the end of the train to safety before their carriage went the way of the first five, but before they could manage it, the coupling linking them to the rest of the train snapped, and the sixth carriage plunged downward into the foaming water. It rolled, floated, buffeted about until it came to rest on a bank of the river about 30 yards from the bridge. The other five carriages also floated way. Most of those who died were in these first carriages. Most survivors were in the three carriages that remained on the bank. Of 285 passengers, 131 lost their lives, and 20 remain unaccounted for.

The lucky ones escaped due to acts of remarkable bravery. Mr Ellis struggled with the occupants of that sixth carriage on the mud bank. As it rolled, one recalled, they were 'floating around, touching people, grabbing at things, but not seeming to get anywhere'. Mr Ellis broke a window in the carriage and with two passengers, John Holman and E J Hartwell, helped to pull people out on to the side of the carriage that remained above the swirling, ice-laden water. Their position was very precarious, for with every swipe of the rapidly-moving river, the carriage lurched and threatened to topple them into the black and seething water. When the 130-ton KA locomotive hurtled into the river, it pulled behind it an oil-laden tender which sailed through the air, landing on the opposite bank where it broke into pieces. The oil spread on the water, adding danger to the struggling survivors, for anyone caught in it risked being smothered, unable to see which way to turn to safety.

The 26 survivors in the sixth carriage managed to form a human chain back to the bank, and one by one made a perilous journey, just a few yards' distance, to safety. The water was flowing so fast that their great fear was of being swept away. Victims recovered the following day had been hit with such force by the water that their clothes had been stripped from their bodies.

Passengers in the first five carriages were not so lucky. In the one immediately behind the engine, a couple and their two children managed to escape through a broken window and struggled to the bank, covered in mud and oil. Another man in the same carriage was swept half a mile downstream before he got any kind of foothold or handhold and crawled to safety. Another survivor described what it felt like to be trapped inside a carriage as it hurtled into the flood:

'Our car went over and we hit the river. We must have rolled over half a dozen times. Mud and water poured in. The car was washed about 200 yards downriver, then stuck on a sandbank and turned on its side. That's what saved us. I smashed open a window and another chap smashed one farther down the car. We pulled ourselves up and held our heads up in the air. There was somebody on the bank and he ran to get help. I think that's how they got to us.'

He may have been spotted by another rescuer, A Dewar Bell, who had been standing nearby and managed to catch four men in turn as they swept by him, within a few minutes of the carriages hitting the water. He stood in the stream and clasped at the bodies as they hurtled by, in great danger himself. Finally he clambered back to the bank, where he saw a carriage that lumbered on to the mud. Five people were sitting on it. He jumped on to the carriage and smashed the windows. There were another 20 people inside. He rescued 16 in total before the waters took their toll. The speed and weight of the water was so strong that remnants of carriages were found the following day two and a half miles away. Only heavy metal pieces remained—wooden superstructures were broken up and borne away in the flood.

The exact cause of the disaster was soon discovered. Above the valley of the Whangaehu River stands the icy peak of Mount Ruapehu, one of New Zealand's North Island volcanoes. In its centre lies a vast crater, filled by a beautiful lake. It is from the foothills of Ruapehu that the Whangaehu flows, so the source of the flood water inevitably lay there. After the disaster, four experienced mountaineers climbed up to look at the volcano and found that the surface of the lake was 25 feet lower than its usual recorded level, and its total surface area, once 14 acres, was now only three acres or so. Fresh mud and blue clay six to eight feet deep was found round the edge of the crater, several thousand feet above the surface of the water. Some of the boulders there were still hot.

The volcano had erupted, spewing forth a great stream of water, mud and rock, and this found a pathway down the shallow rut of the Whangaehu riverbed. As the water and mud thundered down the mountain slope, it gathered greater momentum and sucked up large deposits of earth, volcanic ash, boulders, whole trees and hunks of ice. Mount Ruapehu had shown signs of activity in previous years and now broke through its crater walls with this devastating mudflow or *lahar*. The volcano had last erupted in 1945, so there were large deposits of ash readily available, adding weight and substance to the sudden flood of water and mud.

The bridge at Tangiwai was no lightweight, flimsy structure. The force of the lahar is evidenced by the total destruction of five out of the seven spans, two of 44 feet in length, and three of 22 feet, standing on thick concrete piers. One of these, crumpled like a rotten tree, washed up several miles downstream. The river had been increased, in one sudden moment, to 20 feet higher than its usual volume. Next day when the flood had subsided, pathetic evidence of its power could be seen where remnants of clothing hung caught in treetops along the mud-smeared banks.

Rescue operations were mounted within half an hour of the derailment. Some survivors went to a small forestry service camp at Karioi, four miles away. At nearby Waiouru, staff from the military hospital rushed out to the scene to see if they could help the injured, but very few needed serious medical attention. Those who escaped were shocked, bruised, covered with mud and slime, but for the most part, sound in body. Twenty-one people were treated at Waiouru, 12 at Karioi and 12 at another village in the vicinity, Raetihu.

Rescuers continued with the grisly business of recovering bodies from the mud for days. Identification was difficult because clothing, documentation and other personal property was stripped away by the icy water.

Some few individuals had extraordinary escapes. One woman was found 300 yards from the crash, buried up to her neck in mud with only one arm free. Rescuers dug her out, and she was carried, badly injured, to safety. Other people may have scrambled out uninjured and got away from the scene in a state of shock, possibly taking volunteered lifts in passing cars. They never reported their getaway and made the official task of assessing the disaster more difficult. Twenty people therefore remained unaccounted for when the final figures were released the following April.

One of the saddest aspects of the disaster was that the train was probably more crowded than usual, because it was Christmastime, and because Queen Elizabeth and the Duke of Edinburgh were visiting Auckland at the time. They had arrived there on December 23rd, and the Queen was to make her Christmas Day broadcast from the capital. She expressed her sorrow in her message, and the Duke attended the mass funeral held at Wellington shortly after the disaster. Queen Elizabeth also awarded The George Medal to Mr A C Ellis and Mr J W Holman, while two other rescuers, W I Inglis and A D Bell were given the British Empire (Civil Division) Medal.

The Board of Inquiry found no one to blame for the disaster. Mr Ellis had provided evidence of the driver's attempt to stop the train, but natural catastrophe simply overcame human effort. Speaking of the driver and fireman, Mr Ellis added, 'They were the real heroes of the smash. If they had not applied the brakes and sanded the line, more of the carriages would have plunged into the river.'

Strangely, the disaster did not prevent the reconstruction of a new bridge in the same site. The suitability of the train route and the remoteness of risk outweigh the evident hazard. This 1953 disaster was by no means the first. Sudden floods in the Whangaehu are recorded for 1859, 1861, 1863, 1889, 1895 and 1925. The 1861 flood took away a bridge near the mouth of the river—those of 1889 and 1895 are known to have resulted from volcanic eruptions of Mount Ruapehu. 9000 feet high, the icy volcano stands as a permanent reminder that the forces of nature are unpredictable and contemptuous of human life and endeavours.

Above left The cause of the flood was an overflow from the ice-bound crater lake of the volcano Mt Ruapehu. *Middle left* The force of the water was sufficient to demolish an entire steel structure. Five out of the seven steel spans of the bridge were destroyed. *Below* Debris from the train was left stranded 15 feet above the river's usual height, indicating the sudden violence of the flood. Remnants were found for several miles downstream.

October 9, 1963
Overflow of the Vaiont Dam

Below Two views of the village of Longarone and surrounding countryside, before and after the avalanche of floodwater poured out of the Vaiont Dam.

The disaster of the Vaiont dam on October 9, 1963, was partly man-made and partly natural. A combination of forces led to the destruction of at least eight villages in the Piave valley and caused the loss of 1189 lives, the greatest number of peacetime casualties in Italy.

The cause of destruction was the collapse of a whole side of Mount Toc, a peak rising 6000 feet above the south side of the Vaiont dam. The landslide fell into the great basin of water inside the dam, forcing a giant wave to tip forward over the front edge, so that it fell almost vertically into the valley 870 feet below. A great torrent, estimated at 200 million cubic metres of water, mud, rock and timber, hurled down the valley and destroyed everything in its path. The dam itself remained intact, although at the time it was thought that such terrible havoc could only have been caused by some break in the structure.

As the wave lunged down across the valley, it hit the bed of the Piave, crossed the river and rushed up against the right bank. Here were situated several outlying settlements—hardly villages even—Longarone, Pirago, Rivalta, Villanova and Faè. Longarone was four-fifths destroyed; the others were completely obliterated.

Nothing survived where the floodwater descended. The Treviso-Calalzo railway line totally vanished: not just the train carriages, but station buildings and water towers were swept away. The tracks were ripped up and carted off. A few miles downstream railway lines were found rolled round and round like giant bed springs. Houses of wood and of stone, electricity pylons, even asphalt road surfaces, were all ripped to pieces by the force of water.

The disaster occurred in the late evening, when nearly all the valley's inhabitants were quiet at home, reading, watching television or asleep in bed. There were practically no survivors. The entire valley was transformed in a few minutes into a vast mud and shingle river bed. Bodies were found lodged high in trees where they had been flung by the violence of the wave. The business of recovering the dead was slow and arduous, and many were not dug out until days later.

The few who survived had tales to tell of their miraculous escapes. A doctor in Longarone, Gianfranco Trevisan, was watching television with his family. His house sat on the northern side of the village, high above the valley, and it survived the avalanche:

'The door suddenly burst open; I called my wife and children and shouted to them to run up the mountain. I thought the dam had burst. We were expecting it . . . Several big landslides had fallen into the lake from Mount Toc. Every so often the ground at Longarone shook, only a fortnight ago the ground shook.'

The doctor's servant was among several house-holders on the slopes of Mount Toc who had been given notice to leave their homes a few days before the disaster. Everyone in the valley had known at once what the cause of the flood wave was.

As enquiries into the cause of the disaster began, it became clear that the Vaiont dam had been a source of worry and fear from its beginning. The dam was constructed from 1956–60 and was considered one of the finest large dams in the world. 261·60 metres high, with a curving wall 190 metres wide, its most unusual feature was the double curved shape of its front wall, like an ancient arrowbow. This design was supposed to give it maximum strength, to resist the pressure of water behind, and at the same time create maximum storage volume, thus saving money. In its thinnest part the lip of the wall was no more than three metres thick. The maximum volume of water it could contain was about 150 million cubic metres, exerting a pressure of 65 kilos per square centimetre. The Vaiont dam was the centrepiece of a chain of five constructions forming the northwest Piave hydro-electric system.

This magnificent feat of engineering was beset with difficulties. Cave-ins and cracks appeared in Mount Toc almost as soon as the dam was finished, causing such concern that the lake was not immediately filled. In 1962, authorization was given by local authorities who had been assured that the dam was a safe structure, although many experts still expressed doubts.

The engineers bored into the mountain several yards deep on either side of the dam and reinforced it with concrete. Special sensitive instruments were positioned on the rockface to record any stress, strain or movement in the rock. A survivor, Rodolfo Barzan, had worked on the dams as a carpenter in the early days and knew of the engineers' worries: 'The technicians knew that part of Mount Toc would fall into the lake. They were waiting for it from one day to the next . . . For this reason they often shone lights at the sheer face of Mount Toc'. He then described what he saw on the evening of the disaster: 'I heard a terrible noise, something between thunder and a salvo from an artillery battery. I thought it must be Toc—the lights on the mountainside went out and a terrible wind began to blow across

Below 1,189 *lives were lost in the deluge. The high death toll was due partly to the time of the event: most villagers were at home in bed or watching television when the water hit.*

Above The perimeter wall of the Vaiont Dam, showing the huge landslide that fell into the lake from Mount Toc.
Far left Italian soldiers and civilian volunteers help to identify the bodies.
Left Part of the Treviso-Calalzo railway line vanished in the flood.
Right A few refugees from Longarone leave their partially demolished house carrying a few belongings.

the lake and then came the wave. Then a thick dusty fog rose everywhere. It was dark and you couldn't see a thing.'

If the thought of an accident was so present in everyone's mind, why did the authorities do so little to warn villagers or to take further preventive measures? It must have been obvious that any break in the dam wall or collapse of the mountains around the artificial lake would result in catastrophe. Only the villagers around the dam lake itself were given any kind of proper notification. The Mayor of Erto put up 'notices of continued danger' in the Pineda district as near before the event as October 8:

'Owing to the fact that landslides from Toc could cause dangerous waves on the whole of the lake, everybody but particularly fishermen are warned of the danger of venturing on to the lake shores. The waves could run dozens of metres up the shore, carrying away and drowning even the most expert swimmer.'

One natural phenomenon may have helped to trigger off the Toc landslide of October 9, but it was a final straw rather than the initial cause. There was a minor earthquake in the mountain area just before the face of rock fell. It took place at 10.42; the slide began at 11.15. Seismologists at the Bendandi Observatory at Faenza believe that the strength of the seismic waves showed that strain had been building up inside the mountain for some time.

The force of the landslide changed the landscape of Piave. Not only was the valley floor a massive stretch of mud and rubble, but for a time the Piave River swelled to three times its normal size. Looking back across the desolate scene, survivors saw the wall of the dam still rising sheer and solid, a giant white triangular wedge between two mountain faces. But instead of blue sky above it, a hump of earth, almost a hill, blocked the light. When a helicopter flew over the top of the dam, the pilot saw a new peak rising out of the remains of the lake. At the front edge near the dam wall was a small pool of water; the mountain filled the centre. Only a third of the original lake remained behind the peak. The new mountain had trees still growing, mostly intact, though a few looked a little lopsided, as if there had been a fierce storm. Grass and plants covered the earth between them, and in one place the pilot spotted a small pathway winding up between the trees.

A Government enquiry was set up immediately to find out how such an appalling disaster could have been allowed to happen. Among the many questions which it had to answer was whether sufficient testing and surveying had taken place before the site was selected. One alarming piece of information was the discovery that tests about the suitability of the dam's location were still in progress, three years after it had been completed. The enquiry also had to consider whether the warning notices and partial evacuation of people living around the lake and on Mount Toc should have been taken seriously as an example by the communities living on the valley floor.

When the enquiry published its findings, most of the suspected failing proved to be true. The dam authority, ENEL (the Italian nationalized electrical industry), were found liable for choosing an unsuitable construction site. Various builders and engineers were held equally to blame. Lastly the public authorities in the Piave valley area were criticized for not taking due regard of the dangers and warning their local residents that catastrophe could occur.

May 24, 1964
Lima
Football riot

The riot in Lima football stadium on May 24, 1964, was one of the most bizarre events in sporting history. About 300 people died in the violent fighting and mass hysteria that was produced by a soccer match between Peru and Argentina in the Peruvian capital.

Admittedly, football is a passionate interest among Latin Americans of all classes, but the riot was set against the high tension then running through Peru's political arena as well as the sporting one.

The game was a qualifying match for the Olympic Games scheduled to be held in Tokyo the following year. The Argentine team were in the lead, with the score standing at 1–0. Only two minutes of play remained, when Lobatón, a popular Peruvian winger, scored an equalizing goal. The stadium crowd went wild with delight, but in a matter of seconds their cheers turned to yelps of protest. The referee, R Angel Pazos, a Uruguayan, had disallowed the goal for dangerous play.

The whole stadium was soon in an uproar, and the reaction was so terrifying that Pazos ordered all the players off the field. The game simply could not continue in such an atmosphere, and Pazos was genuinely worried at the inadequacy of police protection for the two teams and himself. They all ran for shelter down a ramp that led out of the stadium.

The riot started. It was triggered off by a well-known football fan, Matias Rojas, nicknamed 'The Bomb.' A thick-set local character, habitué of the stadium, he rushed on to the football pitch to attack the referee. All 40 police and two dogs fell on him and in front of the volatile crowds in the stands, manhandled him and dragged him off. At this, the crowd's indignation could contain itself no longer. With a mighty roar the spectators in the South Stand behind the goal surged forward, leaning and heaving on the iron fence that separated them from the pitch. It gave way, spilling them all over the ground.

The few police on hand had already managed to barricade the players and referee behind the steel door of a locker room, and two hours later they were smuggled out of the city centre.

But innocent members of the football crowd had little chance to get away so easily to safety. Many were trampled to death by the descending crowds. Every window in the stadium was smashed, and fires were lit in the stands—a favoured device of protest among Peruvian football hooligans. The frightened police over-reacted, adding to the pandemonium by lobbing tear gas at the crowd and shooting bullets over their heads. This created panic and a blind flight for the doors, which were all locked. People in front tried to shout, 'There's no way out this way —go back, go back!' but the mob surged forward, forward, so that many at the head were crushed to death or suffocated by the press of bodies. And, the effect of the tear gas on the crowd was acutely painful. One man who rushed up into the stands to get out of the melée felt as if he would choke to death on the gas, so thick was the cloud that arose.

Another man who suffered two broken ribs tried to save his 18-month-old baby daughter by holding her high above the terrified crowd. But he lost his balance and let go of her. She was one of the victims crushed in the crowd against the corrugated iron doors.

The hospitals were soon overloaded with casualties. A temporary morgue was set up, and bodies were laid out on the lawn outside the hospital building where anxious relatives had the agonizing task of wandering about trying to find missing members of their family.

But the events inside the stadium were not enough to exhaust the pent-up emotions of the crowd. Another mob marched on the Presidential palace, tearing down flags from the Plaza San Martin on the way, waving them in the air and shouting 'Justice! Justice!' They wanted to protest to President Fernando Belaunde Terry at the police brutality and to have him intervene officially to have the match declared a draw.

Next day, feelings still ran so high that a third mob stormed the stadium once more, breaking in and stealing trophies and fencing swords from one of the practice rooms. At the university campus a further crowd of chanting students demonstrated, calling for the resignation of the entire cabinet. The student's union called a 24-hour strike.

Out of the crowd of 45,000, at least 300 died and a further 500 were injured. The Government declared a state of emergency throughout Peru and ordered a full investigation of the event. Legislation was rushed through Parliament to give financial assistance to widows and orphans and to pay for the victims' funerals. Seven days of official national mourning was announced.

The funerals began the following day at 9am. Each service was taken individually, unlike the more common practice in other countries of mass burials after such a disaster. The traffic jams created by the mourners stretched for several miles around the main Lima cemetery.

Almost at the same time, the Chamber of Deputies rejected a motion to censure Minister of the Interior Juan Languasco for alleged responsibility for 'police brutality'. And on May 27, the police arrested more than 50 individuals and charged them with looting and incitement to violence. Some had callously robbed victims as they lay dying in the stadium.

A year later, an examining magistrate again called for the trial of the by then out-of-office Minister of the Interior and the chief police officers on duty at the time. In a report submitted to the Peruvian Supreme Court, the magistrate, Dr Benjamin Castaneda, accused them of direct responsibility for the disorders that led to such a severe loss of life. But the Government had given its verdict at the time of the riot: 'left-wing extremists' were to blame for trying to organize

Previous page A policeman with a guard dog looks on as tear gas bombs explode inside the Lima soccer stadium.
Left Spectators scramble higher up the terraces to escape the violence and the fumes.
Above Riot police lob more tear gas in a frantic effort to force the rioting crowds to leave the grounds. At least 300 people were trampled to death.

demonstrations despite the state of siege (a modified form of martial law) that was in effect at the time.

In a report published in the *New York Times* just after the event, American journalist Robert Lipsyte commented, 'In many countries where soccer is one of the few diversions and emotional releases for a poor and restless mass, the game takes on the proportion of a kind of controlled warfare.'

It would be wrong to think that the riot in Peru was a demonstration of a kind of passion found only in Latin countries or poorer nations. There has been a notable increase of violence among sports spectators in many other parts of the world, particularly in England, over the past few years. There were peculiar political tensions in Peru in 1964, but tensions created by lack of money, few job opportunities or mishandled crowd control by the police could cause mass violence anywhere.

Studies into the psychological causes of such hooliganism have received increasing attention in the two decades since the Lima riot as the number of violent incidents rapidly increased. The way violence builds up and the best methods to control it have been the focus of much attention, often with the help of monitoring cameras. Certainly no solution has been found and the barricades, once a ridiculed feature of South American stadiums, are going up wherever the game is played.

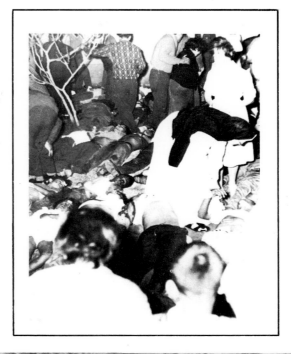

Left *Victims laid out in a Lima hospital waiting to be identified.*
Below *The riot continues outside the stadium. Mobs of youths hurl stones at the police. A further mob stormed the stadium the next day.*

WALES

Aberfan

Cardiff

October 21, 1966
Landslide at Aberfan

On October 21, 1966, the people of Aberfan in the Merthyr Valley of Wales were just starting work when a sound like thunder shook the air. At the edge of the village, a rain-soaked, 800-foot-high heap of waste coal slag slipped, engulfing a school, a row of terraced cottages and a farm. The fall ran for half a mile before it slowed down and covered the buildings like a cold, black volcanic eruption.

A local schoolboy watched: 'It uprooted a great tree on its way . . . two other boys ran the other way. It just sucked them away and they ran right into it. It hit the school like a big wave, spattering all over the place and crushing the buildings. It was like a dream and I was very scared.' One hundred and forty-four people died under the tip, 116 of them school children gathered for morning assembly. Ironically, they were due to break up for half-term at noon that day.

'Our strong and unanimous view is that the disaster could and should have been prevented . . . decent men led astray by foolishness or by ignorance or both in combination are responsible for what happened at Aberfan.' That was the verdict of the Government's public enquiry.

Plenty of warning had been given about the likelihood of such a disaster. The tip was over 30 years old, and debris was still being put on top of it when the accident happened. The men working there in broad sunlight saw the tip begin to slide away, but they could not see what happened because a thick fog obscured the valley below. All they could hear was the sound of trees being crushed.

The tip had moved before: in 1959 and again in 1964. In December, 1939, lower down the same valley at Abercynch, nearly 200,000 tons of coal sludge had slid one-third of a mile and diverted the course of the river Taff. Another tip-slide in the Rhondda Valley 40 years before had caused tremendous devastation. Even worse was the disclosure soon after the Aberfan disaster that Mrs Gwyneth Williams had raised the question of safety at a Planning Committee Meeting as far back as 1964: 'We have a lot of trouble from slurry causing flooding. If the tip moves, it could threaten the whole school.' A former headmaster, W J Williams, had repeatedly warned authorities and villagers of the possibility. One

of the few 'good' results came about instantly—Lord Robens, Chairman of the Coal Board, ordered an immediate check on 500 other tips in South Wales. The National Coal Board estimated that between 100 and 200 other tips were in a dangerous condition at the time.

An almost willful ignoring of danger signs is one of the basic characteristics of man-made disasters. In the face of overwhelming factual evidence, people seem to say 'It won't ever happen'. No one knows quite why this strange attitude develops. Aberfan has a number of aspects common to all disasters. The work done by rescuers reached heroic proportions in length of hours on the job and fervour of volunteers. When an event of such a terrible nature occurs—and barely a family in Aberfan was spared bereavement—a frenetic energy goes into searching for survivors and struggling to clear up. The body wants to push itself to the extreme of physical exhaustion, so that when the realization of the event hits, it will be too tired, too numb to feel the pain. Shifts at two local collieries were stopped, and miners came up from the coal face, covered in black, to work ten-hour shifts. One man whose daughter was believed dead ran three miles to the school and was still digging at six in the evening.

The compulsion that goes into the work effort sometimes creates inefficiency. At times there were 5000 people digging out the school, the terraced houses, the farm and the streets of Aberfan. People had to be restrained because it was impossible to hear a cry from a trapped person amid the noise of all the activity. As the day progressed, traffic and crowd control became severe problems. Police had to seal off all roads. At first, a Territorial Army Sergeant, Ron McCarthy, who had arrived with a squad of 22 men, volunteered on his own initiative to organize traffic control. From about 5pm, he managed to enforce a one-way system to help keep vehicles moving around the village.

Headquarters were set up in a small room at Merthyr Tydfil police station. Eventually, both army and Automobile Association officials were brought in to deal with the stream of traffic into the village. Ambulances trying to get on to the road between Cardiff and Merthyr Valley found their way blocked by a stream of vehicles carry-

Left Pathway of destruction. Long neglected, the Aberfan tip, 800ft high, had accumulated a vast weight of rainwater. On October 21, 1966, the waste and sludge of the precarious pile slid down on the Welsh village in its shadow, killing 116 children and 28 adults, most of them in the village school, which was completely obliterated by the weight of the slide.

ing in pit props, sandbags, shale to make safe temporary roadways, scaffolding materials and cylinders of gas for floodlighting. Men worked round the clock, the whole scene illuminated by the strange white glow of gas lights and the blue flashes of police cars.

Always present was the danger of another fall, because the tip had not only absorbed a large amount of rainwater in the days before, but was also found to have a spring running right under it. Experts measured the flow after the slide and found it was discharging from a single source at the rate of 100,000 gallons per hour.

Coal Board officials claimed that the tip slide was caused naturally by a spring rising up inside the tip. Lord Robens made this announcement three days after the event and was supported by the divisional production director, Geoffrey Morgan, who added that he thought the spring was a recent eruption. Coloured dyes were used to trace the source of the spring and its course. Local people maintained that there was no stream at that site before the tip was started and were more concerned that so few precautions had been taken about the safety of tips in general. This was to be the key issue for the public enquiry.

The problem had started with the onset of mechanical mining in the early 1900s. Coal was extracted from smaller, dirtier seams and vast

accumulations of waste came out of the mines with every ton of good coal. Occasionally this slag was taken back down to fill in disused shafts (more in Europe than in the UK) but more often, artificial hills began to burgeon on the landscape. There were complex safety rules for procedures below ground in the mines themselves, but the tips were seen only as eyesores, and responsibility for them was put in the hands of planning committees rather than safety officers. Attempts were made to develop special grass seeds and to bring in suitable shrubs to mask the blots on the horizon, but rules about maximum height were set by planning committees rather than imposed by safety considerations. There were no firm regulations about inspection of tips, geophysical tests or shoring up of sides to prevent slipping.

These were all matters discussed by the Public Enquiry, set up immediately after the Aberfan disaster and headed by Lord Justice Edmund Davies. Born at Mountain Ash only two miles from Aberfan, he had spent many years as a highly respected lawyer in the valleys specializing in mining problems before he rose to the judiciary. He had been involved in the famous Padola murder case and he tried the great train robbers. When the enquiry was set up, the Attorney-General Sir Elwyn Jones issued an order on October 27 that the press and television were to cease commenting on the Aberfan disaster in any way until the results of the enquiry were published. While many journalists and public figures thought this ban was too strong and infringed the rights of the general public to hear open comment and discussion, it did at least take the public gaze off the devastated village for a while. News reports petered out; the final story dealt with the 10,000 people who attended a mass funeral at Aberfan cemetery for 81 of the children and one mother.

The enquiry proved to be the longest to date in British legal history. It lasted for 76 days, heard the evidence of 136 witnesses and published a detailed report in August 1967. It made absolutely clear where the fault lay and what ought to be done to prevent another such disaster:

'Blame for the disaster rests on the National Coal Board. This blame is shared, though in varying degrees, among the National Coal Board headquarters, the South Western Divisional Board and certain individuals. . . . there was a total absence of tipping policy and this was the basic cause of the disaster. In this respect, however, the National Coal Board were following in the footsteps of their predecessors. They were not guided either by Her Majesty's Inspectorate of Mines and

Quarries or by legislation'.

The report also noted that many of the witnesses had been oblivious to what lay before their eyes. All the danger signs had been ignored, time and time again. 'It did not enter their consciousness,' the report said. 'They were like moles being asked about the habits of birds.'

But the enquiry was at pains to quash the bitter accusations that there had been 'callous indifference' on the part of local Board officials, when people in the village had tried to tell them about their fears of a slide. 'Callousness betokens villainy, and in truth there are no villains in this harrowing story . . . the Aberfan disaster is a terrifying tale of bungling ineptitude by many men charged with tasks for which they were totally unfitted, a failure to heed clear warnings, and a total lack of direction from above'.

One fact emerged from the report which defies belief. It was clearly established that there was no record of any inspector visiting the Aberfan tip for four years previous to the disaster, although this was regarded as part of the regular duty of a mines inspector. No reasonable explanation for this lapse was forthcoming at the enquiry or since.

The report not only laid the blame where the commission felt it belonged, but pointed out

Overleaf One of the nobler aspects of the various reactions to a disaster is the immense capacity of humans to share hard work and grief. Miners from nearby pits worked ten-hour shifts after their jobs in the efforts to dig bodies from the debris. At times there were as many as 5000 people at work around the site of Pantglas school.

some basic steps that it felt should be taken immediately. First, tunnels should be built in tips to provide permanent drainage, to remove the danger of another waterlogged slide. Second, the report approved of schemes to re-contour existing tips that could not be removed so they would blend more into the landscape and not be such looming eyesores for the villagers who have to live in their shadow. The enquiry also looked into the European customs of underground stowing of waste, but came to the conclusion that it could not recommend the practice for British mines. The methods used would make mining in the UK uneconomic, and the problems of airborne dust created by the stowing procedure endangered the health of workers on the job.

As to the policy of having tips largely the concern of planning and environment committees, the enquiry made a strong recommendation that tips should be regarded as potentially dangerous engineering structures and that proper steps should be taken to deal with them accordingly.

Although it was felt that a complete overhaul of the National Coal Board would have to result because communications between various levels and departments had obviously failed, the en-

quiry concluded that control of tips should remain with the National Coal Board.

Its recommendation that a National Tip Safety Committee should be set up was quickly put into effect. The Advisory Committee on Tip Safety was established in 1968 by the Minister of Power. The chairman was secretary of the Council of Engineering Institutions and one member was a mining engineer. There were also three Government assessors working with the Committee which regularly advised the Secretary of State for Trade and Industry on matters concerning the stability of tips. This task later fell to the Mining Inspectorate who answer to the Health and Safety Executive.

The Aberfan disaster produced a number of proposals from other sources. The most important concerned the use or misuse of public money that accumulates at such a time either through voluntary fund raising or the launching of an official appeal.

Public reaction at the time of the Aberfan disaster took several forms, some much less attractive than others. An incredible number of people hampered the rescue effort by gathering into large crowds of spectators. After the event, tourists arrived by the hundred, and police had to check every vehicle in and out of the village to

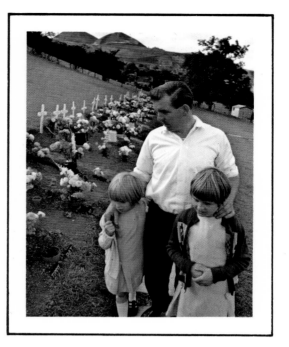

eliminate non-essential trips. Sightseers continued to turn up, haunting the villagers for many months afterwards. The Queen and Prince Philip, who were deeply concerned and wanted to visit Aberfan, had to delay their arrival until October 29 because of the 'tourist' influx. When they did go, it was one of the most informal encounters ever made by the Royal Family. Local Councillor Jim Williams simply invited the royal visitors to his home, and as they passed through the village, The Queen and Prince Philip were introduced to parents along the way. A wreath was laid in the cemetery; there were no official presentations or processions of cars.

Sympathy and shock were seriously felt by the general public, and a disaster fund launched immediately reached £71,000 by October 26, just five days after the event. (The total sum of the fund was finally closed at £1,606,929 on January 31, 1967.) Princess Margaret launched a special appeal for toys to be sent to the surviving village children and received an overwhelming response from the British public.

But the money and the gifts only created dissension among various groups involved in the disaster. In November, it began to be clear that the villagers would have to battle hard to be properly represented on the disaster fund committee. At first two 'rival' groups arose among them, the Parents' Association of people who had lost children or relatives and the Aberfan Residents Association, representing those not bereaved but concerned about the future life of the village. They soon joined forces under the co-chairmanship of Reverend Kenneth Hayes and Mr Tom Lewis, and eventually got five members on a committee of 15 in January 1967. The general atmosphere of bitterness and frustration about what to do with the money was increased by the strange inertia that set in. Months went by without concrete plans, and no money went to the village it was intended to help. The appointment of a fund administrator in the following May at a salary of £3,000 did little to help; feeling increased that the money was only going to be misused. The pressure for an immediate shareout of the fund gave the world outside a rather misleading impression of the Aberfan villagers as materialistic or self-seeking.

As a result of this embarrassing and painful controversy, Jeremy Thorpe, Liberal MP, introduced a bill in the House of Commons to set up a National Disaster Fund to cope with the understandable public desire to send money at such times of suffering. The function of the fund would be to ensure that a proper amount of money was spent on the right remedies.

The bill was introduced on March 20, 1967, but was not enacted. Another proposal came from Lord Robens, who suggested there should be a permanent disaster force with special vehicles maintained on a regional basis to provide telephone and telecommunication systems and round the clock canteens for the rescue workers. This has not been put into practice either, although a

Above left Immediately after the disaster, the National Coal Board ran a safety check on all other tips in South Wales and found between 100 and 200 were in an unsafe condition.
Above Tips are created from the waste matter that is a by-product of coal mining. In some countries this waste is stowed underground, but this procedure can be a danger to the health of the miners. One result of the tragedy at Aberfan has been better control and regular examination of all tips.
Above right The worst scars of the Aberfan tipslide stay with the survivors. Hardly a family escaped the effects of bereavement.

similar scheme was established in 1974 by Mrs Judith Hart, Minister for Overseas Development, to help cope with foreign disasters.

By far the worst aspect of the Aberfan disaster was the effect it had on the villagers themselves. With all the money, rebuilding and world-wide sympathy, the long-term suffering continues. A psychological study was conducted with the co-operation of the villagers and was published five years after the tragedy. Seventy-three adults and 85 children took psychiatric treatment, although many more who needed it did not go for help. Both children and adults still suffer nightmares; some young ones have experienced such a deep shock and sense of alienation that they make friends with difficulty and dislike going out. The most appalling feature of the villagers' grief was that everyone suffered. There were few to comfort and give strength who were close enough to be of use. So Aberfan turned in on itself. One or two families suffering bereavement can be helped by neighbours and drawn back into ordinary life; at Aberfan the whole village was trapped in loss. The effect on the generation of parents has been worse than for the surviving children, who have more future and fewer memories.

In spite of the sorrow, less than a dozen families chose to move out of the village, and most of those only went to a new estate not far away at Merthyr Tydfil. As often happens when a disaster of this nature occurs, people did not run away but stayed to build life anew. With the disaster fund, Aberfan built a magnificent new community centre, to which the Queen made a promised return visit in March 1973, composed of a concert hall, a swimming pool, squash court, hobbies and games rooms. In Her Majesty's words 'It looks to the future and stands as a symbol of the determination that out of the disaster should come richer and fuller life.'

November 4, 1966
The Florence flood

Senor Piero Bargellini tells a story about the flood that swept through the city where he was mayor on November 4, 1966. A citizen woke early in the morning and looked out of his window at the massive swirl of water filling the streets below. 'I know that Bargellini promised to clean up Florence,' he mutters to himself, 'but I think this is carrying it a little too far.'

That comment is typical of Florence and its people's reaction to the disaster. There is a strong tradition of civic pride and independence, and a general scepticism about the effectiveness of bureaucratic power. The events of the 1966 flood showed all these elements clearly.

Rainfall and flooding in northern Italy that autumn was especially heavy. An annual hazard, these floods caused damage over a 36,000 square mile area. In the 24 hours before Florence was hit, more rain fell in the northeast area than is usually recorded in six months. The valleys of the Po and Arno rivers were the worst affected. Altogether, 112 people died, 11 were reported missing and 5000 families were left homeless. Twelve thousand homes and farms in the countryside and 10,000 houses in towns were destroyed. Hundreds of bridges were swept away. Farm equipment was severely damaged, and industrial areas, especially in the hinterland of Florence, were washed out.

Internationally, the greatest impact was made by the news of the devastation in Florence itself, where centuries-old palaces, crammed with rare works of art, lay defenceless in the path of the River Arno's flood water. In the evening and early morning of November 3 and 4, the river rose 18 feet higher than usual. When the Arno reaches flood level, its two main tributaries, the Mugnone and the Affrico, increase the swell. The first place where the water can gush out over its banks is in the city of Florence. The old part of the town, a cluster of thirteenth and fourteenth-century houses and palaces lies just alongside the river as it runs through the heart of the city. Between the famous churches of Santa Croce and Ognissanti, world famous museums and galleries like the Uffizi, the Museo Bardini, the Museo delle Scienze and the Biblioteca Nazionale stand shoulder to shoulder along river embankments and narrow side streets. Parapets, frescoes, beautiful arched bridges such as the Ponte Vecchio and tiny shops full of Florence leatherwork, gold jewellery and glass complete the most beautiful art centre in the world.

By 2.30 in the morning of November 3, signs of impending disaster could already be seen in the city. Drains were overloaded, with spurts of water shooting up through the gratings in the gutters. The Arno, usually a sluggish stream well down the steep embankments built protectively along its sides, was turning into a boiling surge of dirty water. Cellars along the river banks were already being flooded, yet no official alarm was given. It had been decided by the authorities that too early a warning would cause panic and was unnecessary in any event.

The only people who had any advance news were the goldsmiths and jewellers from the old quarter on the Ponte Vecchio. Some families had been in business there for generations. Loyal nightwatchmen telephoned their employers when the Arno began creeping up the arches of the bridge. Several shopkeepers drove through the torrential rain to save as much of their stock as they could. Afterwards, there was bitterness among the citizens that a few were fortunate enough to be informed, while the majority lost their entire livelihoods.

At about 4am, the full force of the floodwater began to descend on the city. All the morning people worked frantically to move their furniture, vauluable possessions, everything, to the upper storeys of their homes. In the museums and art galleries, a near-hopeless task of rescuing priceless works of art began at dawn. About 7 o'clock, the staff of the Uffizi gallery rushed to work and started carrying oil paintings up from the basement and ground floor. Among works saved were paintings by Filippo Lippi, Masaccio, Giotto, and Botticelli. Over 300 were moved to safety.

In the Museo delle Scienze, the curator, Maria Luisa Bonelli, was all alone. She tried to save the rarest of the museum's pieces, including Galileo's telescope, by carrying them through a second floor window into an adjacent building. The greatest damage to a work of art occurred at Santa Croce, a beautiful thirteenth-century church with a fine cloistered courtyard. In the old refectory, a crucifix painted by Cimabue was torn from its place and thrown into the swirling mud and water. It was 70 percent destroyed, a loss for which no realistic monetary assessment can ever be made. Cimabue was one of the finest late 13th-century painters, a teacher of Giotto and one of the last Byzantine stylists in Italy. Only a handful of his works remain, and the Santa Croce crucifix was considered one of his best. In the Piazza del Duomo, the cathedral square, the famous 'Door of Paradise' belonging to the Baptistery was ravaged by the flood. The two fronts are covered in 20 gilded panels, carved by Lorenzo Ghiberti between 1403 and 1453. Five of these were torn off and hurled about in the filthy water, which at times reached a speed of 80 to 90mph.

All morning, the flood water surged over the banks of the river, over the tops of the oldest bridges, gushing through shop windows, hotels, churches and palaces. Oil drums, dead cows, trees and cars were carried through the town by the force of the flood. As it swirled through basements and cellars, it broke open central heating systems and added the most destructive element to the muddy swirl: oil. Naphtha and other chemicals in the water did irreparable damage to oil paintings, mosaics, delicate ancient frescoes and wall carvings. When the flood eventually receded, a thick black slime of mud and oil clung to the walls as high as the tops of doors.

Apart from works of art, the most serious damage to Italy's heritage was the loss of thousands of rare books and manuscripts from the National Library. Monks at Santa Croce saw black, oily lumps floating in the water as it filled the church courtyard almost to the top of the cloister arches. These were rare leather-bound volumes, sodden, stained and falling apart under the impact of the water. 300,000 books were damaged or lost, 24,000 manuscripts, 705,000 letters and other documents and 68,000 musical works. Sadly, many of the books had come from libraries well outside the flood area for restoration and repair in the Florentine workrooms.

Although few people lost their lives in Florence itself, the suffering among the citizens was great, especially as no relief plan or proper rescue facilities materialized until days later. The hospital of San Giovanni di Dio was hit at about 8am. When its basements filled with water, the generator stopped and the hospital soon became freezing cold and sodden. Patients had to be carried up flights of stairs, wrapped in blankets, into crowded, candle-lit wards. At San Salvi, the mental hospital, patients became terrified by the rising water, but nothing could be done to calm them, as the hospital's medicine supply had been ruined in the flood.

In the Santa Teresa prison, panic spread fast, and 80 of the 200 inmates escaped in a mass break-out. Many dived off the roof into the swirling water. Some were recaptured; some went straight to their villages in the countryside to make sure their families were safe. Others were commended for bravery after the disaster for volunteering themselves in rescue efforts. One was recaptured months later in a hillside village outside Florence, where he had been posing as a film producer looking for locations.

In central Florence where the flood did its worst damage, 100,000 citizens were marooned on rooftops without food or adequate protection from the cold. In the late afternoon a lone army helicopter circled over the town, lifting a few to safety.

In the countryside around Florence, help was not so speedy. Many people had been spared the frightening spectacle of the flood because November 4 was a national holiday: Armed Forces Day. Some Florentine families had gone away, so the town was much less crowded than usual. The anger and disbelief of those left behind can be imagined when the national radio network failed to broadcast any news of the flood for most of the day. Instead an endless churn of military marches and high-minded speeches descended on their ears.

By the next morning, November 5, the floodwaters had subsided, and shopkeepers struggled silently through ankle-deep mud to discover the extent of the damage to their little stores. The real disaster for Florence was to its livelihood. Its museums and galleries attract hundreds of thousands of tourists who bring fifty million lira

Below *Shops, cellars and cars are submerged under the floodwater. At its height the water reached over the tops of doors at ground-floor level.*

every year to the city. Yet Florence was poor and had no reserves to take proper precautions against such calamities as large-scale flooding. In the late nineteenth century the city had been provisional capital of a newly-unified Italy. Its palaces had been taken over as administrative or public buildings. No money since had ever gone into an organized plan for restoring Florence to its historic splendour. Paintings, books, sculptures and other rare objects were chaotically stored in bad conditions. The flood added to the general disarray which had long existed as a result of governmental indifference.

Military headquarters in Florence were among the first to take effective action. Soldiers were stationed through the two-thirds of the city damaged by the flood to prevent looting or other forms of civil disorder. But for the most part, the citizens moved about responsibly and quietly, trying to restore normality. Priests organized food distribution centres and performed courageous feats, helping to free trapped people and comforting the injured or dying. In the country-side, the Communist party, which has a strong following in Tuscany, set about restoring water supplies and food and acquiring medical necessities. All the local services worked side by side, not always with superb co-ordination from the top, but with great success at local level. Mean-while government ministers and departments competed in the political game to be the 'single

force that saved Florence' and became hopelessly bogged down in their own rivalry. As a typical example, it was only after six days that the govern-ment sent in machinery and engineers to help clear the 60,000 tons of mud and rubble from Florence's streets. Until that time, the city had only 150 pumps to clear buildings of water, and it took a whole day for one pump to empty one base-ment. Yet four days after the flood, Rome radio announced, 'Florence is returning to normal'. The local newspaper retorted, 'What normality'? Its editor, Enrico Mattei, wrote an open letter to Italy's President, describing the lamentable lack of official help:

'There are some pumps in action, but almost all of them have been brought in from the countryside by private citizens . . . the task of cleaning up the city is virtually at a standstill . . . situations like the one now existing in our city cannot be dealt with by ordinary admini-strative methods'.

Where central government was tardy, inter-national response was immediate, from experts, officials and ordinary people. Students from all over Europe went to Florence and worked long, unpleasant hours in the museums and libraries, salvaging rare books and helping to save paintings. In the Biblioteca Nazionale, they worked in chains, passing up buckets of mud, and retrieving rare volumes. Sometimes the air was so foetid

Below *The Piazza Mentana, Florence. The force of the water swept whole cars, cattle corpses and oil drums through streets.*

with the stench of oil and materials rotting in the slime that they had to wear protective gas masks.

Galleries in London—the Tate, the National, and the Courtauld Institute—sent supplies of mulberry paper which is used to restore damaged pages. The young volunteers interleaved the books, which were then rushed to centres all over Italy, to brick-firing kilns, tobacco-curing sheds and other large drying places. An American student described how readily people worked from dawn till dusk, and how the citizens responded: 'The Florentines brought us bread and meat, cheese, brandy, chocolate and wine. You want to give everything to help to the point of sacrifice'.

Various international loan organizations were set up to help the Florence relief work. Between November and the following January, the USA donated $2·5 million in goods, services and cash. A Committee to Rescue Italian Art was set up especially to care for the restoration of the 300,000 books damaged in the Biblioteca Nazionale, while a separate Anglo-American Relief Fund undertook to provide funds so that the small shopkeepers who had suffered could be put back on their feet. Another fund was set up in the UK in November; by December 19 the British had donated nearly £150,000, with a Government grant of £20,000.

The Italian Government at last announced measures to help raise money within the country for the relief of flood-stricken areas. A special 10 per cent increase was added to income tax and greater levies on petrol, cigarettes and alcohol helped to raise the estimated £287 million needed to cover costs. This figure did not include the many long-term improvements that were soon suggested from all sides to prevent a recurrence.

In the welter of public discussion and recrimination that followed, one shining example of mismanagement stood out. Above the city of Florence stands the hydro-electric dam of Levane, 35 miles up-river. It is run by the Italian electricity authority, ENEL (Ente Nazionale Energia Elettrica). On the day before the flooding of Florence, it appeared that the Levane was near its fullest possible capacity. The exceptionally heavy rainfall could not be contained by the dams along the Arno. Higher still, the La Penna dam was already brimming and had let out an unusually large gush of water, which in turn caused difficulties at Levane. Around 9pm on November 3, the gates of Levane were opened and an enormous volume of water was allowed to join the rapidly rising Arno, speeding towards Florence.

ENEL argued that the extra water from the dam was only a minor factor in the rising flood water. The chief blame, they asserted, was due to the increasing flow from the Arno's tributaries. To outsiders such arguments seem peculiar. The authorities in countries like the UK, the USA, Australia or New Zealand measure the maximum volume in a dam or the maximum rise of a main river. But such data is in alarmingly short supply in many other countries, including Italy. ENEL were quoting figures as low as 13 cubic metres

with reference to the dam excess, compared with 250cu.m. from the rivers. But their figures were based on the dam's normal capacity, and no one knows how much extra water it was holding when the gates were opened.

The technicians at the dam did inform the civil engineers that the floodwater was being released, and they notified the police and the prefecture. No one can be sure whether the real significance of the act was made plain, or whether any urgency was communicated. What is clear is that the right message did not get to the right people, and Florence slept peacefully while the Arno swelled up and fell upon it.

Ironically the city's newspaper *La Nazione* carried the news in its early edition about 7am but few people were around to read it, and by the time they were, the copies had been washed away. 'The city is in danger of being flooded', it reported. 'At 5.30 this morning water streamed over the embankments ... Many families are evacuating their homes ... there are indications that the day ahead may bring drama unparalleled in the history of the city'.

Along with criticisms of the ENEL and the city authorities for failure to co-ordinate activities and warn the people, many suggestions for disaster prevention soon came forward. The most obvious improvement seemed to be rebuilding the embankments of the Arno to withstand future torrents. More reservoirs were requested to cope with the heavy rainfall that so often threatens the area. The long-term ecological view held that it was important to reverse the policy of tree-felling and indiscriminate grazing on the slopes of the Appenines behind the city. When land is weak, overused and bare, water and soil run off unheeded into streams and tributaries. With reforestation and careful farming, the earth acts like a giant sponge, absorbing a good proportion of heavy rainfall.

However, these remedies were all long range, and the citizens of Florence had a well-founded scepticism as far as the central government's ability to turn plans into actions were concerned. Although Italy is a unified nation, the traditional autonomy of its cities still colours attitudes and actions. In Florence, recovery from the 1966 flood was best made by independent local effort, and government planning from Rome had a limited effect. A leading Italian writer, Nicola Adelfi has explained the problem neatly:

'On the one hand we have a society which is mentally anticipating the future with all the impatience of a man who has just realized that his present home is poky and unhealthy and is determined to move into a modern and comfortable apartment—and on the other we have a national economy that is creaking and archaic'.

In spite of administrative problems, Florence made a speedy recovery from the flood. On December 21, 1966, all the city's museums and galleries re-opened with the exception of Santa Croce. The longer work of restoring went on

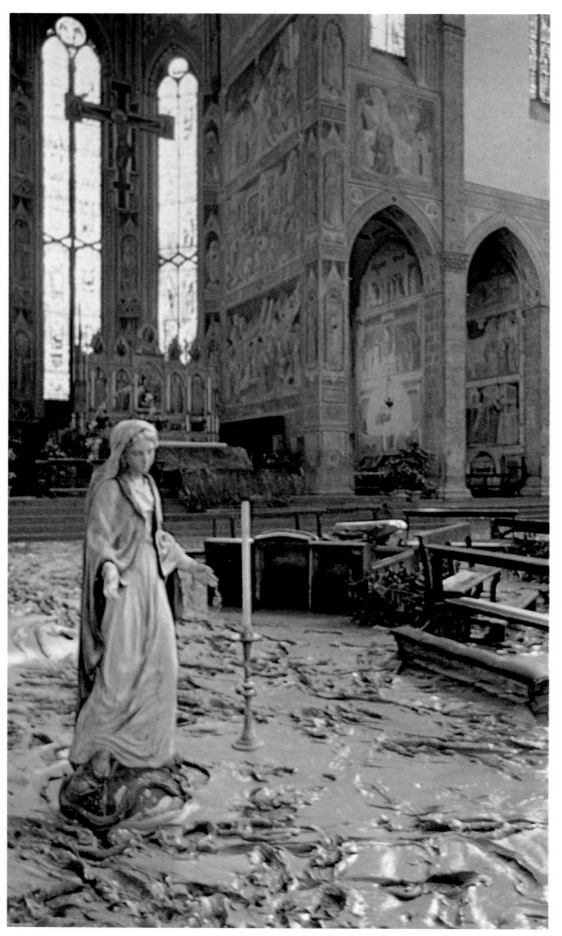

Left *The Basilica of Santa Croce, site of the worst artistic loss of the Florence flood. A pensive Virgin stands amid the slime and mud left behind. The basilica was under 15ft of water at the flood's crest, but miraculously the frescoes by Giotto in the chapels to the right of the altar suffered only minor damage.*

Above right *Some of the damaged shops on the Ponte Vecchio, Florence's famous old jewellery quarter.*

Below right *Thousands of volunteers, many of them students from all over the world, helped in the salvage operations that followed the floods. 300,000 soiled and broken books were among the priceless treasures eventually restored by these dedicated, and unpaid, workers.*

behind the scenes. The former hothouses at the Pitti Palace were used as headquarters for the operation because it was possible to maintain a moist, even atmosphere there. Water damage causes wood to swell and crack, and if canvas dries too quickly, it shrinks and causes paint to flake. The hothouse solved both problems.

Work still continues on the treasures of Florence after twenty years, particularly on the books. At the time it was estimated that it would take a decade and cost a minimum of $1 million. As for the people of Florence, they too made every effort to return to normal. In December, all but 31 of the city's 259 hotels re-opened, and most of those were ready for the tourist season of 1967. Out of the 5000 families made homeless, 500 still had not been rehabilitated by the end of 1966. The leaden Italian bureaucracy tied up public rehousing money for months. One thousand of those offered accommodation were given one room for each family. A hundred or so temporarily took over empty houses in their irritation with the authorities, but slowly these issues were resolved.

Towards the end of the year the government made outright grants of about £287 to small shopkeepers who could prove they had suffered flood damage. In the countryside, all farmers got a lump sum payment of £52, and unemployed labourers received 40p a day until they found jobs. By the end of 1966 all 635 industrial plants in the outlying districts of Florence were once again fully operational. Finally, in December 1966 the government approved a budget of £115 million for rebuilding embankments along the Arno, updating flood warning systems and instituting soil conservation programmes.

Ermenonville

Paris

FRANCE

March 3, 1974
The crash of the Turkish DC10

The DC10 crash at Ermenonville near Paris on March 3, 1974, was the worst in the history of civil aviation. The plane, operated by the Turkish national airline Turk Hava Yollari (THY), had arrived in Paris from Istanbul with 117 passengers aboard. There, 217 others joined the flight. Many of them had been booked with British Airways to fly to London, but changed flights because of a strike by groundstaff at Heathrow Airport. The DC10 left Paris on the normal scheduled departure route, climbing up to about 12,000 feet as it headed northeast across France. Suddenly a violent noise indicated decompression and a new sound began in the plane's engines. The plane zoomed forward with increased speed and, 1 minute and 17 seconds after losing internal pressure, plunged to the ground in Ermenonville Forest It was just five miles from the new Charles de Gaulle airport, where an 11,000-foot runway would have been available. As it fell the plane disintegrated into hundreds of fragments, cutting a swathe 3000 feet long through the trees and scattering bits of luggage and bodies everywhere.

There had been no radio message from the aircraft to say that anything unusual had occurred. The only clue to the cause of the crash came from the French northern regional control centre, where at 12.42 officers had seen two specks on their radar screens; one moving, one stationary. The moving dot could have been the aircraft, the motionless one various items falling from the aircraft, including the rear cargo door and two passengers in their seats, later found a great distance away from the final resting place of the rest of the wrecked plane.

Three hundred and thirty-four passengers and 12 crew members were killed instantly. Rescuers, who took three hours to reach the site because of its inaccessibility, found debris and bits of bodies scattered for miles. No single air crash had caused such high mortality before. The highest death toll previously confirmed was from the crash of a Royal Jordanian Airlines 707 on January 22, 1973, at Kano, Nigeria killing 171 people.

An investigation board to determine the cause of the disaster was established at once. The crash took place on French soil; it was therefore the responsibility of French authorities to look into the facts. A board headed by René Lemair, the inspector general for civil aviation for the Secretariat General, Civil Aviation (SGAC), allowed American and British experts to join, representing the various interests involved. A separate American team from the National Transportation Safety Board came to give their expert help as technical advisors.

The discovery of the cargo hatch cover at the start of the wreckage trail immediately led to speculation that the cause of the crash was decompression due to failure of this door. It had happened before: on June 12, 1972, another DC10, operated by American Airlines, had developed decompression when the cargo door fell off at 11,750 feet and the rear cabin floor buckled in the resulting outrush of air. This in turn jammed the

Number 2 engine cables running under the floor, while the door had smashed into the port tailfin as it ripped away, damaging its mechanism. It was due only to amazing skill that the pilot, Captain Bruce McCormick, turned the plane around and, by using only the ailerons—the levelling control devices on a plane's wingtips—landed at Windsor, Ontario, without further mishap.

Within days of this first suggestion about the cause, some disturbing facts about the Turkish DC10's history emerged. These have helped to turn the crash into one of the worst examples of top level mismanagement and disregard for public safety that has been seen in a multi-national high-finance world such as civil aviation.

DC10s were then a new class of aircraft, the wide-bodied jets, and along with the Boeing 747 jumbo and the Lockheed TriStar, carried half the world's long distance passengers. In 1974 a total of 31 airlines were flying 128 DC10s. The THY plane was one of a batch of six originally ordered by the Japanese Mitsui Corporation, who failed to complete the purchase. Instead the six planes were sold to THY and Laker Airways. The planes' manufacturer was the American firm of McDonnell Douglas, formed by merger in 1967. One of the most profitable companies in the business, the firm has a reputation for excellent design and safety in production.

But a central mystery remained unanswered, and the finding of the French enquiry on this point was eagerly awaited. After the Ontario crash, the American National Transportation Safety Board sent various recommendations to the Federal Aviation Administration, the official body governing the operation of aircraft in the USA. The NTSB wanted certain modifications made to the DC10 and hoped the FAA would issue an 'airworthiness directive' which would have legally required McDonnell Douglas and all DC10 operators to comply with the changes required. But no directive was issued. Instead McDonnell Douglas were allowed to send private 'service bulletins' to all companies that had bought the DC10, suggesting various alterations. None were as basic and crucial as those the NTSB had requested. This in itself was a peculiar state of affairs: bulletins are not compulsory, whereas directives are, and the alterations seemed vital for a safely operating DC10. Even stranger was the discovery that the aircraft sold to Turkish Airlines came out of McDonnell Douglas' own factory after the bulletin was issued without the modifications being made to it. McDonnell Douglas President John Brizendine has said, 'This is a circumstance to which we do not yet have an explanation'. Both the THY and a Laker airplane had records stamped by the same persons in the factory, and they had since moved from their jobs.

What were the key modifications required by the National Transportation Safety Board? Most important was improvement of the cargo door. After the Ontario crash, the NTSB looked at it

Previous page The scene of the DC10 crash, in the forest of Ermenonville near Paris. The force of the plane left a littered trail of wreckage through the trees for several miles.

closely and found that the locking mechanism could operate defectively. If the handle was forced, the door gave the appearance of being firmly closed and engaged an electrical safety circuit so that no warning light flashed on the pilot's control panel. But in fact, it was possible for the 'teeth' on the lock to be only half in place. When a plane with an unlocked door climbed to about 12,000 feet, air pressure inside would build up and force the door open. The impact of the escaping air would be enough to buckle the floor of the cargo compartment, damaging vital engine cables running beneath. It could also cause such swift decompression that luggage, seats and passengers might be sucked out through the hole.

From May 1972 to October 1973 McDonnell Douglas and the NTSB had a long correspondence over changes to be made to the door, and the firm periodically issued bulletins requesting operators to make modifications. The NTSB wanted the door altered so it could not be forced. The compartment is used to stow late baggage, and it often happens that a junior airport crewman is responsible for closing it and might do so inexpertly. Also, the NTSB wanted special 'relief vents' built between the cabin and the cargo compartments to lessen the effect of pressure and to prevent the dramatic buckling effect that damages the controls if the plane is de-pressurized.

These were the requests passed to the FAA by the NTSB. The FAA have stated that they believed McDonnell Douglas' own service bulletins were making sufficient changes to cope with the problems without the need for a directive. By August 1972 various bulletins had been issued, ranging from ordering a special window to be placed in the door so that the locking device could be checked to adding notices outside the door giving detailed instructions how to close it. The NTSB seemed reasonably satisfied by these steps, but continued pushing for modifications to the venting system and to the positioning of the essential engine cables under the floor. In March 1973 the FAA informed the NTSB that McDonnell Douglas were still considering these changes but might not find them 'feasible'. In early 1974 the FAA were still awaiting McDonnell Douglas' views on the matter.

For its own part McDonnell Douglas were reluctant to have any of the changes made by FAA directives. There would undoubtedly be bad publicity for its comparatively recent design, and the company believed that the DC10 was as safe as it could be, given existing knowledge in the field of big jets. If the FAA wanted research done into the general area of wide-bodied aircraft, McDonnell Douglas felt it should be government-funded and industry-wide. There was no reason, as far as the management could see, why they alone should carry the task.

McDonnell Douglas now faced the biggest lawsuit to date in the history of civil aviation. A number of passengers' relatives sued the firm for negligence in its home state of California, where damages awarded could run to millions of dollars.

The DC10 crash brought to light yet another source of confusion and controversy: unlike sea or rail travel, where passengers had responsibility for their own insurance cover and the carriers were not liable in cases of death through negligence, in America airline companies could be held responsible. McDonnell Douglas were not admitting negligence in the matter of design, but did admit that the cargo door was not modified before it left the factory. However, they counter-claimed against Turkish Airlines for negligence through its agent, the cargo handler who closed the door.

Unfortunately, the position of the bereaved relatives in the lawsuit depended on the convention to which their country belonged. The Warsaw Convention of 1929, updated in 1966 in Montreal, could give claimants up to £30,000 damages. Turkish Airlines were not party to the Warsaw agreement, though France and the UK were. The amount of damages depended on various conditions, such as the point of departure. A relative might claim as much as £30,000 under the Montreal agreement or as little as £4362 under the original Warsaw convention with other sums and rules between. Settlements reached in July 1975 in the United States were agreed and paid at the higher US rates.

Three days after the crash the FAA did issue a firm directive to all DC10 operators. The modifications previously requested by McDonnell Douglas became mandatory for all DC10s in service. The complicated legal battle highlighted the need for a comprehensive international agreement about the legal position of all passengers, operators and plane manufacturers and a tightening of insurance regulations.

Below *Three hundred and thirty-four passengers and 12 crew died instantly in the crash. Many relatives came to the scene shortly afterwards to pay their respects to the dead.*

Left *The plane's body fragmented when it crashed to the ground. A sudden loss of pressure occurred when a baggage compartment door which had not been properly closed flew open in mid-air.*

Above and below right *The tedious and grueling task of gathering together remnants of personal possessions was necessary so that a complete list of the passengers could be compiled. Hundreds of police and military personnel combed the forest for several days after the crash.*

OHIO ● Xenia

USA

ATLANTIC OCEAN

April 2 and 3, 1974
The 'Ohio' tornadoes

Wednesday and Thursday, April 2 and 3, 1974 saw the worst tornadoes in the American Midwest since 1925. From Decatur, Alabama, to Windsor, Ontario, across the Canadian border, a series of about 100 tornadoes or 'twisters' as they are popularly called struck no less than 11 states. Within eight hours, 324 lives were lost and $400 million in property was destroyed, enough damage for President Nixon to declare five states as disaster areas.

Mortality and damage were probably increased because some of the worst hit areas lie outside the region where tornadoes most commonly occur. In the 'tornado belt' of the Midwest, where twisters are commonplace, the populations are better educated about basic safety precautions and structural design is more likely to allow for

tornado activity. Xenia Ohio, which suffered the greatest damage, had only experienced seven in the last 24 years, and Brandenburg Kentucky, hit almost as severely, had none in the same time period.

What is a tornado? Usually localized in their effects, 'twisters' cover 200 yards to a mile in area at one time and create a path from five to fifty miles in length, travelling at speeds up to 75mph. The terrifying nature of tornadoes is their unpredictability. They can double back on themselves, take sudden turns left or right or even go round in circles. In the USA they usually affect the Gulf and Midwestern states. The 1974 tornadoes were unusual in travelling so far from south to north, in so short a time, and so far to the east. Tornadoes most frequently occur be-

Below *Traffic on a highway in Cincinnati speeds on its way in an attempt to drive out of the path of the tornado hovering above. This was one of a series of nearly 100 'twisters' that hit the American Midwest in April 1974.*

tween March and July, and statistics put them most frequently between 4.00 and 6.00 pm.

Tornadoes are formed by the peculiar weather effects created when hot air masses from the Gulf of Mexico meet cold polar air masses from the Rocky Mountains that cross into the Midwest. The hot air is trapped beneath a blanket of cold air and cannot rise in its usual way. Sometimes the hot air finds a 'hole' in the blanket and swirls upwards, making currents as it goes. It also cools as it rises, forming clouds and eventually rain.

If this action is rapid then great disturbance soon develops, with dark skies, swirling rain and wind, hailstones and thunderstorms. Static electricity is produced by the great mass of energy.

At this stage people on the ground can recognize the warning signs of a tornado—a looming black cloud hangs high in the sky, sudden gusts of wind shake trees and walls and the air temperature increases ominously, becoming clammy and close. The minute the 'vortex' of the tornado appears, destruction is near. This whiplash tail or funnel-shaped spiral of whirling air is the centre of the tornado's energy. As soon as it touches the ground, the partial vacuum at the heart of the vortex and the fierce whirling winds literally suck up and blast apart anything in their path. An American expert describes the effect of these terrible forces: 'bark has been peeled off trees, harnesses have been stripped off horses, and clothing has been stripped off people leaving them completely naked. Dead sheep have been found shorn of their wool, feathers have been plucked off chickens . . .'

In Xenia, Ohio, the worst-hit town in the 1974 disaster, whole buildings were ripped apart and left like piles of matchsticks. As a tornado passes over a building, the near-vacuum or low pressure area in its funnel exerts a great tug on the rooms below, where the air is of a higher pressure. This air is forced upwards and outwards, blowing the house apart with all the force of a dynamite explosion. Half of Xenia was levelled in this way. Metal street signs were bent back on their poles like flags frozen in a double fold. A van stood in a deserted street—undamaged but for every window blown out clean. A truck was lifted out of a driveway, forced into a tree which it uprooted, and put down upside down on top of it. A train passing through Xenia at that fatal moment was loaded with a consignment of brand new Mustang cars. Every one was dented and full of broken glass. Days later, bundles of bank notes from the smashed bank were found 200 miles away at Cayahoga Falls.

One Xenia family found a vivid example of the tornado's capriciousness in the laundry room of their house, destroyed except for one wall. Splintered wood had been driven through the metal clothes pole; the clothes dryer had been jammed with flying dishes. But an open box of soap powder stood undisturbed on top of the washing machine, exactly as it had been left.

William Hitchcock, a Xenia jeweller, could

Below Splinters of wood litter the ground for miles around destroyed homesteads in Hanover, Indiana, which suffered more damage from the tornadoes than had been felt there in 50 years.

point to the exact time the tornado hit: the hands of the clock in his street sign, bent and twisted, stood still at 4.40pm. 'It sounded like a fast passenger train. It was really just filling the air with stuff, really violent.'

Another Xenia citizen saw the dark cloud in the distance:

'Then all of a sudden it must have touched down. There was a whole mess of confetti going up from the ground. A warm rain started and I knew it was time to go.

'I went into the house and just then I felt the wind kick. We—there were seven of us—got down on the floor of the kitchen . . . then all the windows went all at once, you could hear them breaking all over the house. Then all I could hear was the wind. Mud and glass were flying around and hitting everybody. The rushing wind went on and on. All you could hear was the wind'.

When this man crawled out of his house all the roofs were gone and almost no second storeys were left on any of the houses around.

When the tornado had passed by, people emerged and began picking at the wrecks of their homes, as if gathering firewood, dazed and totally silent. Some just sat. One elderly lady wrapped in a blanket sat in a rocking chair. The roof had blown off her house, but she would not move nor speak for several hours.

The path of destruction across Xenia, nearly one mile wide and three miles long, had been scythed through in five minutes. Out of the 25,000 population, 30 people were dead and thousands homeless. Gas, electricity and telephone services were cut off: dangerous live wires hung from twisted pylons and poles.

The injured, numbering at least 80 were taken to Miami Valley Hospital in Dayton ten miles away; and Ohio's National Guard soon moved in with bulldozers, emergency rations and medical supplies to restore order as soon as possible. Three-quarters of the town's electricity supply was restored by the next day. With contemptuous disregard for the homeless, nature sent a snowstorm to the town on April 5, immediately after the tornado had passed.

The picture of destruction in Xenia was repeated across all the eleven states affected. Alabama, Kentucky, Ohio, Indiana and Tennessee were all declared disaster areas, making massive federal aid available for immediate rescue and rehabilitation programmes, and low-interest loan systems were devised to help businesses.

Kentucky was almost as badly afflicted as Ohio. Seventy-one people died in the state, 29 of them in the small Ohio River town of Brandenburg, 32 miles west of Louisville. Between six and seven thousand homes in the vicinity were made uninhabitable or completely destroyed. Brandenburg itself almost totally disappeared. In Louis-

Below Within eight hours, 324 lives had been lost and $400 million in property had been reduced to rubble. President Nixon declared five states official disaster areas.

ville, the roof was ripped off a school building, and the engine lifted out of a car parked outside by rotational winds estimated at speeds of 200 mph. Much greater tragedy would have ensued if the town's several thousand schoolchildren had not gone home just before the tornado came. Most of the dead were children playing outside.

In Kentucky, insurance claims were estimated at $81.5 million, and Governor Wendell Ford described it 'probably the most tragic day in Kentucky history'.

Indiana lost 22 lives, and many of its smaller population centres were wiped out, like Depaun, home of 500 people. Borden, Hamburg and Martinsburg were 60 percent destroyed. In Fountainstown, eight houses and a fire station were obliterated and a metal frame manufacturing factory's warehouse was lifted off the ground and carried a mile away.

A similar incident caused the death of a man in Virginia when the wind picked up his mobile home, hurled it 100 yards and deposited it upside-down in a wrecked heap. His wife was thrown clear, but suffered some injuries in her fall.

The state of Indiana was severely affected in the south around Hanover, and at Rochester and Monticello in the north-central part. Damage to this area was estimated at $100 million. In Monticello, an elderly lady estimated that the tornado took less than one minute to cross the town.

Above left The whiplash tail of the tornado is the centre of the storm's energy. As soon as it touches ground, the partial vacuum at the heart of the vortex and the fierce winds suck up and destroy everything in its path.
Below Victims of disasters are often stunned and incapable of action while they mentally digest the full impact and reality of what has happened to them.

Left *This mother in Xenia, Ohio was reunited with her three children 17 hours after the tornadoes struck. Many victims of disaster will not accept that relatives or close friends are safe until they can actually hold them and get physical reassurance.*
Below *Reputedly the first-ever photograph of a tornado, taken about 1880.*

'When it had gone I lost everything. My furniture looks like a pile of firewood', she ended.

The National Guard in Indiana had to divert 1000 men to the task of keeping out sightseers, who hampered the relief work. Every truck in the state left in working order was commandeered to help distribute needed supplies.

In Alabama, there was widespread destruction of main lines of communication. The town of Jasper lost most of its main street, its city hall was demolished and its stone courthouse left in a dangerously shattered state. A radio announcer at the local station told his audience: 'We can't talk to the police department—it just blew away.'

There seems very little that could have been done to prevent this widespread destruction. Since the early 1950s, tornadoes have killed an average of 123 people a year. The National Oceanic and Atmospheric Administration said that it had given as much warning as it could, but the unpredictable nature of tornadoes means that they cannot be controlled or prevented.

Ohio was one of the states affected by the last severe tornado strike, on Palm Sunday, April 11, 1965. Thirty-seven separate 'twisters' struck the Midwest, killing 271 people and injuring 5000 more. In 1931 a tornado in Minnesota carried an 83-ton railway carriage and its 117 passengers 80 feet through the air and dropped them in a ditch. Worst of all was the March 18, 1925, disaster, when one single giant tornado ripped through Mississippi, Illinois and Indiana, killing 689 people and injuring hundreds more.

There is very little anyone can do to protect a building that falls right in a tornado's path. The safest place is in a basement or 'storm cellar' specially constructed for tornado shelter. If you are caught in the open, your best chance for survival is to lie down in a ditch or the deepest hollow available. The driver of a car can sometimes steer out of the path of a tornado, but if the vehicle is actually caught, it will be reduced to scrap metal.

If there is no time to get to shelter, the safest place in a building is away from windows to avoid injury from flying glass, and underneath a strong piece of furniture such as a bureau or table which can provide some protection from missiles of debris. Doors and windows on the side of the house facing away from the tornado's path can be left open to try to equalize the pressure, thereby reducing damage to the building. It is never advisable to take shelter in big open-area buildings with weak roof structures, like school gymnasiums and indoor swimming pools.

The only preventive measure that gives any real hope of lessening the destruction caused by tornadoes is to improve the early warning system, so that people are given time to get to shelter and can be kept informed about the path that a tornado is likely to take. Just before the 1974 disaster, the National Oceanic and Atmospheric Administration had asked Congress for an extra $16 million to do just that.

Below The funnel-shaped cloud of another tornado rips its way across Texas. These killer winds, which can reach a speed of 400 mph, are particularly prevalent in the Midsouth and Midwest, especially in the months between March and July.

ENGLAND

Hull

Flixborough

June 1, 1974
Explosion at
Flixborough

Twenty-nine people died and more than 100 were injured when the UK's worst industrial explosion devastated the Nypro plant at Flixborough, near Scunthorpe, on June 1, 1974. One hundred homes in the village were destroyed or badly damaged, and the force of the blast was so great that it could be heard 30 miles away. The Nypro plant was gutted by a fire that broke out immediately following the explosion and raged uncontrollably all day. It was still burning 24 hours later. Only eight badly charred bodies of the 29 dead could be recovered; 27 were Nypro employees, another a sub-contractor and the last an outside driver who happened to be at the factory when it blew up. The disaster occurred late on a Saturday afternoon when a reduced staff of 70 were on duty. Otherwise the death toll could have been enormous, for the firm employed a total of 550 people.

The explosion caused widespread surprise since chemical factories built on this massive scale were supposed to be so well protected in building design and safety procedure that accidents of this sort could not happen. Immediate clues to the cause came from the reports of a few eye witnesses.

Tom McCale, a chemist technician working in one of the labs saw a flash and then glimpsed flames licking along a trail of leaking gas. He shouted to his seven colleagues to get out, and they all ran out of the lab in one direction while he turned another way, right into the force of the explosion. He suffered serious concussion and was taken to hospital.

Another worker who escaped from the part of the plant where the explosion originated, Area One, was Lawrence Harry: 'I heard a bang, quickly followed by a large explosion. Everything went black as hell. I was picked up and thrown 30 yards. We were wandering about in a daze. One of our friends was missing so we went back inside to get him.'

From outside the plant, descriptions from onlookers give some impression of just how devastating the blast was. One man in Scunthorpe, six miles away, told how 'it parted the clouds and went up like a mushroom as though an atom bomb had exploded'. In the village of Flixborough roofs were torn off houses, windows blown out and walls cracked. People in the street were badly injured by flying glass imbedded in their flesh, so violent was the impact. Some were picked up and hurled against walls or cars. A local housewife expressed the shock of most of her friends: 'It went up like an H-bomb in mushrooms with two circles. I never expected anything like this. I never realized there was such a danger.'

Her comment sums up public reaction to Flixborough. The villagers around the Nypro plant had never been told about the process or its inherent risks.

Nypro Limited was owned jointly by the British National Coal Board and the Dutch State Mining Company—Holland's equivalent to the

Previous page Acrid fumes and uncontrollable flames pour out of the Flixborough Nypro plant. An explosion in which 29 people died was caused by a leaky gas pipe.
Left The blast blew out windows and injured several people in nearby villages. The local inhabitants had little idea of the potential danger on their doorstep.

Above left A road sign on the outskirts of the village stands bent by the blast, which could be heard 30 miles away. Most of the homes in Flixborough suffered some damage.

Below left Fire-fighting efforts were hampered by the deadly fumes that poured out of the chemical containers. It took firemen more than 24 hours to get the fire under control.

Above A scene of devastation at Flixborough. Ironically, no one from the village worked at the chemical plant. 3000 people were evacuated for fear of a further explosion.

Right Luckily the blast occurred on a Saturday afternoon when a reduced staff of 70 were on duty. Otherwise the usual work force of 550 people might have been present.

NCB. The Flixborough plant was the single manufacturing centre in the UK for caprolactam, a key ingredient in the manufacture of nylon. The history of the plant exemplifies modern industrial development through competition. The British firm of Courtaulds had been excluded from the expanding field of nylon manufacture because its rival ICI and the American giant Du Pont had a firm grip on the only known process for making nylon fibre, patented 'Nylon 66'.

Then in the early 1960s, the Dutch State Mining Company found a new way to make almost the same product, which they called 'Nylon 6'. At first they went into partnership with Fisons, an English fertilizer company, who were interested in a by-product of the new process. But as DSM improved its methods, this by-product was reduced in quantity, and Fisons dropped out. DSM then turned to a similar organization as its new partner and the NCB stepped in.

At that time the joint venture was supplying Courtaulds with 20,000 tons of caprolactam, the chemical used to make nylon. The National Coal Board became 45 per cent owners in May 1969. Gradually the process was simplified and speeded up until at the time of the accident the plant produced 70,000 tons a year, an annual output worth £18m. However, greater hazards crept into the process. The plants operated by DSM under licence in North and South America used a slightly longer system, but from 1973 the Flixborough plant involved a short cut, using benzene rather than cyclohexane to start the process. It is cheaper, but it is also highly toxic, inflammable and explosive.

The crucial moment in the manufacture of caprolactam comes after the benzene has been used to produce cyclohexane. This chemical is then mixed with ammonia in an oxidizing plant. The cyclohexane is under great pressure at this stage, and the supply of oxygen must be very precisely controlled. What comes out is cyclohexanone oxide, which is treated with concentrated sulphuric acid or phosphoric acid at the isomerizing plant. This produces caprolactam, which in turn produces 'Nylon 6'.

From all accounts it looked as if the explosion had resulted from a leak in a gas pipe which ignited immediately. Cyclohexane is like petrol in the safety problems it presents; 1000 tons were stored at Flixborough at the time. Regular precautions included searching employees for lighters, cigarettes and matches, and issuing special footwear for use in certain areas of the plant. But, as one expert pointed out, even the static electricity created by wearing a nylon shirt on a warm day could provide the spark to cause a fire if there was an undetected leak.

Although the explosion caused more death and damage than any previous in peacetime, it did not come totally unheralded. In September 1973 Brian Harvey, the chief inspector of factories, had published the annual report of the Inspectorate and gave the following clear warning in his introduction: 'We may well see a continuing fall in the fatal accident rate, while at the same time we are faced increasingly with the risk of failures which could result in multiple deaths and injuries of near-disaster proportions.' As a result of Mr Harvey's recommendations, a new bill 'Health and Safety at Work' was on its way to becoming an act of Parliament at the time of the Flixborough explosion.

Its proposals seem so commonsensical that it is cause for wonder that nothing of the sort had become law before. The prime task of the bill was to reform the jumble of long-standing rules and regulations that cover industrial hazards, many of which date back to the middle of the nineteenth century. At least six different Government authorities watchdog factory building and operation. Industrial plants, mines, agricultural sites, nuclear installations and explosives manufacturing are all separately governed. The bill sought to put all these together in one uniform organization. It also provided that employers should inform their work force and people living in the immediate vicinity about the nature of possible hazards and the degree of risk involved. Unions would be empowered to place representatives on a factory safety committee, to put forward the workers' opinions and express any fears.

Something at least was being done, but another area of doubt and confusion was opened up by the Flixborough disaster. The plant was the sole UK supplier of caprolactam. It provided the basic raw material for an industry employing 30,000 people, making goods as varied as nylon stockings, carpet backing, seat belts and tyres. All these jobs were threatened by the closure of the plant. As there was a world shortage of caprolactam supplies anyway, there was little chance of the manufacturers affected being able to switch their orders to other plants. In one day, June 3, Courtaulds lost £20 million off its stock market value, because it was one of Nypro's biggest customers.

Industrial experts argue that giant-scale operations like Flixborough are a good thing. They are cheaper to operate than numerous small factories dotted about, because they cut down transport and manufacturing costs. Raw ingredients can be bought more cheaply in bulk. They provide a job centre for the areas where they are located. But these arguments look only at the economic and business factors, not at social or environmental ones. Flixborough changed that. The validity of building giant plants that can wreak havoc if they explode or allow harmful chemicals to escape is being questioned. Even in pure economic terms, the disastrous consequence of losing a complete supply of a raw material at once, never before taken as a likelihood, is causing serious re-thinking.

One important fact about the Nypro plant is easily overlooked. In Flixborough, population 300, no house was without damage, yet no one from the village worked at the plant. It has always been a quiet, rural community. After

Aberfan, parents protested the decision to leave remaining coal tips where they were; at Flixborough, a local committee was set up to prevent another monster being built in place of the twisted metal ruin. The plant gave off small chemical explosions for a week after June 1. The Flixborough disaster brings into sharp focus the problem of placing a potential hazard near a community which reaps no direct benefits from its presence.

After the initial assessment that a broken pipe allowed a gas leak that caused the explosion, a four-man enquiry headed by Roger Parker QC was set up to look into the overall problem of safety in large-scale plants and to make recommendations. It was to consider whether it is better to have gas-filled pipes passing through the open air so that leaks can dissipate harmlessly into the atmosphere, or where, because of the risk of ignition and explosion, such pipes should be built inside thick walls to contain any blast. More research was needed, including a properly-funded experiment.

Industry and technology move forward quickly, sometimes without full realization of possible hazards to society. Plants and factories cannot be built in deserts. After Flixborough, other installations, such as oil refineries, even airports and big garages, were looked at in a more critical light as potentially dangerous. As Inspector of Factories Brian Harvey commented, 'We are running instead of walking. We have to feel our way with these new technologies'. Ten years later the chemical disaster at Bhopal in India showed that this lesson has not yet been fully learnt.

Above right The Flixborough explosion brought into question the wisdom of large-scale factories. This disaster knocked out the only source in the UK of caprolactam, a substance essential to the manufacture of all kinds of nylon goods.

Right Only eight of the 29 bodies could be recovered from the wrecked plant, so intense was the force of the explosion and the heat of the fire that followed.

CARIBBEAN SEA

HONDURAS

CENTRAL AMERICA

PACIFIC OCEAN

November 18, 1974
Hurricane Fifi

A giant hurricane swept through Honduras in Central America on the night of Wednesday, November 18, 1974, causing 8000 deaths and destroying the homes of another 10,000 people. The disaster, the greatest of its kind ever to afflict one country, could not have happened in a more unfortunate place. Honduras was virtually a disaster area before Hurricane Fifi arrived. It is the poorest country in the Americas, with a rapidly growing population. The average worker earns no more than about £80 a year.

There had been signs of hurricane build-up off the coast of Honduras two weeks before, but no harm came to the land area that time. When the national radio broadcast heavy rain and high winds warnings in the evening before Fifi arrived, some people did not give the message its real significance. Then, in the dead of night, the hurricane tore up the east coast of Honduras, with winds of up to 140mph smashing the poorly-built houses of farm labourers and torrents of rain dropping 24 inches of water in 36 hours.

The worst hit area was around the town of Choloma where nearly 3000 people died. By Friday morning the dense rainstorms had created an avalanche of flood water. Trees, mud and boulders tore down the Choloma River and destroyed nearly all houses on its banks. Over half the citizens of Choloma died. One survivor, an old man of 76, lost all his family; when he searched the ruins of his home, he found two strange bodies washed into it in a bank of mud. 'I don't know who they were,' he said. 'They were just poor innocents who were swept down the mountain and ended up here.'

More people were killed by the floods and other hazards that followed Hurricane Fifi than by the force of the storm-wind itself. In the area around San Pedro Sula, the second city of Honduras in the northeast of the country, 400,000 people were left homeless and prey to exposure, starvation and disease. So great was the threat of an epidemic of typhoid (endemic in Honduras anyway) that the government ordered the immediate mass burning of bodies to prevent infection. In Choloma about 2700 dead were incinerated. The town was an appalling sight, with bodies lying about in the mud rapidly putrefying in the intense heat that followed the rains and winds of the hurricane. There were other natural hazards too, like snakes and spiders, for fer-de-lances and tarantulas wriggled out of their natural homes in the undergrowth in banana groves, disturbed by the flood waters.

Bananas bring in half of Honduras' foreign exchange, and the giant plantations, mostly owned by American companies, employ 30,000 people. A whole year's crop was destroyed by Fifi, an economic disaster matching the human one in magnitude and severity. Huston Lacombe, manager of the United Fruit Company's Honduran subsidiary, described his company's losses: 'We have 28,000 acres of bananas. Twenty thousand are under water, and five thousand were flattened by winds. The waves lifted the railroad track from its bed on the plantations around La Lima [on the coast] and the company's wharves at Puerto Cortés were badly damaged'.

In the Aguan valley plantations, mostly owned by the Standard Fruit Company, another American concern, were totally destroyed. Floodwater spread seven miles from the river bed itself. The total loss to banana growers in Honduras was estimated to be as high as $150m.

These two companies followed their stated intention and rebuilt their plantations, although the disaster had brought fears that they might pull out altogether. Further, because Honduras was so desperately poor, the President, General Oswaldo Lopez, had been making firm demands on the largely foreign-owned companies in order to raise taxes. Now, in addition, they faced heavy costs for re-establishing their industry and for re-opening the railway that carried the fruit from the farms to the coast for shipment abroad, which they owned at the time. In the event, because Honduras was producing 13 per cent of the world's bananas, the big fruit companies could begin business again on their own terms, not those of the government, despite the country's dependence on this agricultural industry.

What about the surviving victims of Hurricane Fifi? Their fate was to suffer even greater hardship after the disaster. Many were stranded for days, clinging to rooftops, sitting in trees high above the flood, waiting for rescue. Help was long in coming because all bridges, roadways and electricity supplies were wiped out. After a couple of days, American helicopters arrived from bases in the Panama Canal Zone, and in one rescue effort in the countryside around San Pedro Sula, 34 refugees scrambled into a helicopter with normal maximum capacity of 15.

Far left The scene of destruction in Choloma, Honduras, in the wake of Hurricane Fifi. Some 8000 people lost their lives in the worst hurricane ever recorded in the western hemisphere.
Left A satellite weather track of Fifi shows the enormous size of the storm gathering over Honduras.

109

Gradually food and medical supplies began to arrive in the stricken areas. Two towns were appointed relief centres: Tocoa, 125 miles northeast of the capital, Tegucigalpa, and San Pedro Sula, in the middle of the area worst affected. Rations came from the USA, Great Britain, Mexico, Cuba, and the Central American states nearby. But the threat of starvation was becoming a reality for many. American Ambassador Philip Sanchez commented: 'You ask how people can starve in just three or four days, but these people were hungry even before the disaster.'

The hurricane not only destroyed rich banana groves but also the meagre little strips of farmland where the fathers of large families in constant want of food eked out subsistence crops. A Honduran relief official, Lt Col. Eduardo Andino, said, 'People are starving, their supplies were washed away and there are no stores near their villages. They have no way to get food except from us.'

Heated accusations began to fly about in the first weeks after the disaster. It was suggested that the Honduran officials had exaggerated the number of lives lost in Hurricane Fifi in order to get more money from foreign aid sources for the languishing economy. The plight of Hondurans alive or dead is so sorry that no amount of over-estimating could produce unfair or unnecessary sums of money.

Yet worse stories emerged about the conduct of the relief programme. The Honduran army was in charge of the operation, and at times came into conflict with the international organizations trying to run emergency canteens and field hospitals on the spot. Soldiers and Red Cross workers battled over supplies arriving at the airport in San Pedro Sula, as frequently happens in developing countries where corruption and crude political tactics combine to use food and essential medicines as bribes or valuable stockpiled capital. (The same problem arose with the north Andes earthquake, Peru 1970, and the 1972 'quake at Managua, Nicaragua.)

At a local level, efforts to organize relief were muddled and varying in success. In some of the refugee camps that sprang up in a matter of days, central food distribution and canteens proved futile because families persisted in their usual habit of cooking for themselves. Most useful equipment was lost in the mud. The Honduran government had neither the resources nor the expertize to organize a rehabilitation programme on the required scale. There were no bulldozers, cranes or flying doctor outfits, and no emergency stores of food or medical supplies.

Cuba provided one of the most immediate and effective remedies: a field hospital team of about 40 doctors, nurses and orderlies, who set up headquarters in a cattle market. A small stadium there was used to provide beds on stone seats. The main work of the team was to provide immediate injection services to prevent epidemics, simple first aid and food for the injured.

Above left The Tela railroad, privately owned by American banana-growing companies, was washed out by the floods that accompanied the storm. Most of the banana plantations, which grow the major part of the export produce for the whole of Honduras, are situated near San Pedro Sula, the worst-hit town in the country.
Below left At La Ceiba, Honduras, a house carried downstream came to rest precariously astride a damaged bridge.
Above In Choloma 2700 dead bodies had to be incinerated to lower the risk of disease and infection spreading in the sweltering heat that followed the hurricane.

Great Britain sent in troops from nearby Belize and gave army supplies of blankets, camp beds, ten-day rations kits and medicines. £20,000 was sent from the British government, and efforts were co-ordinated through the new Whitehall Disaster Unit under the Ministry for Overseas Development, the first time that the new organization had been put into full operation.

The USA sent helicopters and planes that flew supplies to isolated outlying areas. Peace Corps workers soon had camps and kitchens set up in a more orderly fashion. An international disaster fund was opened to provide money on a long term basis for the work of rehabilitation.

It was estimated that it would take Honduras at least two years, with foreign aid, to recover. But that would allow only for a return to the position existing before Hurricane Fifi struck. To better the state of the tiny nation would take far longer. For example, the lack of sufficient numbers of relief workers was brought about in part by the fact that the Honduran government would not relieve army garrisons on guard duty along the border with El Salvador. Honduras had a short but disastrous war with this rich neighbouring country in 1969. Afterwards she withdrew in protest from the Central American 'common market' and damaged her own chances of economic and social progress, an action which had disastrous effects.

Perhaps the saddest aspect of the disaster was that the peasants of Honduras probably did not see that some of the blame should lie with political factors, not natural forces. Maria Hernandez, a 54-year-old survivor from Choloma, said in a filmed interview just after the hurricane that she thought the disaster had come as a judgement from God. People were not working hard enough and did not have the right attitude. Her own daughter had been swept away by the floodwater; her last words had been 'God forgive me'.

A belief in divine retribution is common and deepfelt at the time of a catastrophe. After a few days or weeks more realistic and critical reactions set in. However, over 10 years after Hurricane Fifi, Honduras is still the poorest country in Central America, with official neglect of the problems of the poor and increasing involvement in the political turmoil of the region.

Above left *In San Pedro Sula, some inhabitants piled their meagre possessions on the roof of their abandoned houses.*
Below left *A distraught father carries his half-drowned child to safety in San Pedro Sula.*
Above right *International Red Cross workers were among the first to arrive to help the stranded, sick, homeless and hungry.*
Below right *An estimated 50,000 people were left without shelter after Hurricane Fifi.*
Most Hondurans live on the brink of starvation under normal circumstances, with little physical stamina and no reserves of food or money to help them through such a crisis.

December 3, 1984
Chemical gas leak, Bhopal

The sheer enormity of the chemical disaster at Bhopal in central India is hard to comprehend, even harder to convey. Some 2500 people died and as many as 200,000 suffered injuries, often of long-term duration.

The accident occurred at night, at about 1 am on December 3, 1984, when some 45 tons of toxic gas leaked from a pesticide factory. The gas spread over a densely populated area killing hundreds as they slept. Tens of thousands took to the streets, running to escape the deadly cloud which rolled along near the ground. As they fled their eyes streamed, they coughed and choked and found it hard to breathe. Blinded by the fumes they stumbled into each other in the dark. Many more died on the road. There was panic and confusion. No one knew what to do or where to go. They did not know the source of the gas or what it was.

Lack of information and indeed basic knowledge was an important contributory factor throughout this tragic accident and its aftermath. Most people in Bhopal did not know that lethal chemicals were stored at the factory. The local community certainly had no emergency procedures for such an eventuality. When people reached hospitals the doctors had not been told what the gas was and so could only treat the obvious symptoms. Worse, when they were finally told, in some cases several days later, that it was methyl isocyanate (MIC), there was little knowledge of the effects of this substance and no known specific treatment.

In any case local medical facilities were overwhelmed by the numbers affected. The gas had drifted over an area within about a 4.5-mile (7km) radius of the factory. Thousands came in all kinds of vehicles and on foot. Over 60 hours after the leak occurred more were still coming. Tents were erected in the grounds of the hospitals and special medical posts set up. Doctors did all they could to alleviate their suffering and saved many lives by the promptness of such treatment as they were able to give. But thousands died in the days that followed, while thousands of others remained grievously injured in hospital.

The immediate effects of the gas, which had strong primary irritant properties, were on the respiratory tract and the eyes, particularly the cornea. The cause of most deaths was originally thought to be pulmonary oedema, a condition which induces drowning in body fluids accumulated in the lungs, but evidence from post mortems suggested that poisoning by some form of cyanide, resulting from conversion of the MIC, may have been responsible. It was thought at first that many thousands of people would be permanently blind, but although many continued to suffer with eye problems no cases of total blindness were finally recorded. Babies, young children and the very old were the most susceptible to the gas; some sources give up to half of the deaths as children. Medical specialists from various countries flew in to give help.

Previous page: the gas leak at Bhopal shattered the lives of thousands of families, striking down adults, children and livestock.
Right: an accurate count of deaths was never achieved due to burials in mass graves and long-term fatalities, but the number was known to be well over 1200.
Inset: Union Carbide's unit at their Institute, similar to the one at Bhopal. They closed down their plant in West Virginia as a result of the Indian disaster.

Above: *Shenaz Raes was eight months pregnant when the leak occurred. Inhaling the gas caused her to go into premature labour, and she, like so many others, has since suffered further complications.*

Although numbers have been given, because of mass burials and cremations and later deaths from long-term effects, no final death toll may ever be known. Large numbers of people continued to suffer for months, many for even longer, from eye irritation and respiratory problems. The health of everyone affected was to be continuously monitored for signs of long-term damage.

A massive relief operation was undertaken. The local community was devastated. Bhopal, the capital of Madhya Pradesh state, is an industrial town with a population of about 700,000. The area worst affected was the low-lying old city where the poor neighbourhoods are situated, the wealthier districts being in the surrounding hills. People had run towards the hills to get above the cloud of gas, which was heavier than air and so stayed low. The town was cordoned off and trains, planes and road vehicles stopped from entering. Thousands continued to leave, however, heedless of assurances that everything was now 'safe'. On the streets, many had dressings on their eyes and the sound of coughing was ceaseless. They queued hopeful of relief at open-air clinics where oxygen was given from cylinders. The carcases of thousands of dead animals including cows, goats and buffaloes lay in the streets, the leaves on the trees had yellowed and many plants had withered. The effect on livestock and crops in the long term was unknown.

Families carried their dead to the mortuaries but these were overflowing and mass burials and cremations were held. House to house searches revealed buildings in which everyone inside had died. Particularly badly hit was Jayaprakash-nagar across the street from the factory, where many lived in shacks of mud, thatch and rubble. The tiny, packed dwellings had been turned into gas chambers.

The source of the gas was a chemical factory owned by Union Carbide India Limited (UCIL), a subsidiary of Union Carbide Corporation, the US-based multinational. It started operating in 1980 and was welcomed by the town as it brought about 800 jobs. Its location, only half a mile (1km) from the railway station, about 3 miles (5km) from the town centre and surrounded by a densely populated residential area, was at least contrary to existing safety guidelines. Increasing numbers had gravitated to the area because the work was there, putting up shanty dwellings as near as possible to the factory gates. The plant was licensed by the Indian government and the licence had been extended for a further seven years in 1983, iron-ically after UCIL had apparently agreed to get improved technology from Union Carbide to enable it to handle emergencies such as gas escapes.

The factory produced pesticides for agricul-ture, using methyl isocyanate as an inter-mediary chemical in the manufacturing pro-cess. Union Carbide also used it at their plant in West Virginia. It was not classified as a hazard-

Above: over 3000 cattle were killed by the gas, and workers had to struggle to dispose of the carcasses before they caused an epidemic of disease.
Left: a map of Bhopal, showing the proximity of the Union Carbide plant to the city centre.

ous air pollutant on the US Environmental Pol-lution Agency list, but there were stringent rules about skin exposure in the US plant and, because it was known even in small doses to cause 'unbearable irritation' to eyes, nose and throat in 'minimum time', people living any-where near that factory were warned to stay in-doors with a wet towel over their face in the event of a leak. No such warning was given in Bhopal.

MIC is made by combining methylamine and phosgene. Because of the effects of the escaped gas in Bhopal, particularly the lung injuries and the damage to plant life, some experts thought that phosgene had leaked too. Indeed, a year after the accident exact knowledge of what gas or gases leaked was still hindering medical treatment. Those who inhaled the gas on the night of the disaster described it as having a pungent smell like chillies cooking. In many cases this is what woke them up and so saved their lives.

The gas leak had occurred in one of three underground tanks storing MIC at 15 degrees Celsius. MIC is liquid up to 38 degrees Celsius and very volatile. The tanks had three safety devices: a valve, a vent-gas scrubber and a flame tower. However on December 3 there was a runaway reaction due to contamination of the gas by water, a consequent build-up of pressure, and the safety systems were inadequatee to contain it. About 45 tons of the gas, together with liquids and solids pushed out by the reacting mass, escaped in 45 minutes before the leak was plugged. The accident happened at the weekend, when the plant was understaffed and there was little supervision.

A judicial enquiry was set up by the state government, which also filed a case of criminal negligence against UCIL and took the factory records. The plant manager and five workers were arrested. Union Carbide began its own investigations into the cause of the accident, but when the company's investigating team arrived the police would not at first let them into the factory, and they arrested Warren Anderson, the chairman of Union Carbide, when he arrived in Bhopal. He was charged with causing death by negligence but was released on bail and returned to the United States.

The question of safety at the factory was not a new one. Workers had repeatedly warned of leaks and bad safety procedures. In 1982 they had pasted up thousands of posters in Bhopal which began 'Warning – save yourselves from death'. In the same year a report at Union Carbide, made public after the accident, had revealed problems with valves and 'major concern' about workers' exposure to toxic materials. But Union Carbide management insisted that Bhopal was up to the same standard as their US plant although their own safety inspectors have been quoted as disagreeing.

Meanwhile in Bhopal, about a week after the disaster, when the number of deaths each day was beginning to drop, there remained a pervading sense of anxiety. People were afraid and angry, and had no faith in the safety of the plant or in anything the authorities told them. There were known to be stocks of MIC still stored at the factory and, when it was announced that it would go into temporary production on December 16 to get rid of the remaining 15 tons, thousands left the city on packed buses and trains and in cars. The authorities stressed there

was no danger and that some of them would be present at the factory to prove it, but they provided transport and camps outside the town for those who wanted to leave. In a determined evacuation, an estimated 150,000 went in the three days prior to the 16th. Many thought the temporary camps still too near and went on to villages further away.

Bhopal was quiet and deserted around the Union Carbide plant where, in the narrow streets, shops and houses were padlocked against looters. 'Operation Faith' as it was named, in the hope that it would restore the people's trust, took several days. Elaborate, visible safety measures were taken to reassure those remaining that everything possible was being done. After this the factory was closed indefinitely with the consequent loss of jobs.

Claims for damages against Union Carbide running into billions of dollars were filed in the United States, the first only a few days after the accident. US lawyers specializing in personal injury had gone to Bhopal and were much criticized as 'jet-set ambulance-chasers cashing in on tragedy'. The Indian government, on behalf of all the victims and their relatives, filed claims against Union Carbide in the United States and in India.

Where the claims were heard was important because awards for damages are considerably higher in the United States. In this respect the 'ambulance-chasers' probably offered the best help available, in spite of the American practice of payment by results which would mean at least 30 per cent of any award made. But they asked no money in advance and there was nothing to pay if they lost – important considerations to the poor, especially in families who had just lost the breadwinner. So, with help from Indian associates, they signed up many plaintiffs.

However, claims for compensation depended on the cause of the disaster and who was found to be legally responsible. In March 1985 Union Carbide published its account of the accident, describing it as 'the result of a unique combination of unusual events'. On the important question of how the water got into the tank, the report said it could have been introduced 'inadvertently' through a valve linking the tank with the atmosphere through which nitrogen was thought to have been escaping, or 'deliberately', thus hinting at sabotage. Indian scientists reporting on the same problem believed that a temporary bypass pipe authorized by Union Carbide, combined with a valve which was faulty due to bad maintenance, had let water in during a pipe-cleaning operation the evening before the disaster. This view was supported by the Indian government. Information in both reports revealed that there were faults in the design of the factory's safety system which could not cope with a runaway reaction, although this was a known hazard of storage of MIC when the plant was built. They also blamed errors by local operators as a contributory cause.

In 1988 an 'independent' judgement from an American consultancy called in by Union Carbide denounced the pipe-cleaning theory and gave the cause of the accident as sabotage by a worker who had deliberately let water in to the MIC tank, which would absolve Union Carbide from legal liability.

However, after over three years of protracted legal wrangling, the case had not yet even come to court and, shamefully, the people of Bhopal had received no legal compensation. They were caught between the multinational and the government, both of whom could, and should, have done more for them 'without prejudicing their case'. Thousands still suffered from their injuries, many unable to work, and there was no social security. Some said they had battled against death from MIC to face starvation instead. Bhopal needed the investment and the jobs which the factory brought and it needed pesticides if the alternative was no food. But above all it needed to be given full knowledge about what it had imported, and a government with the ability and responsibility to regulate it effectively and safely. The design and location of the factory could have been better and safer. People died or were injured on an unprecedented scale because of ignorance.

Above: water being handed to victims as they awaited treatment outside a local hospital. The queues were vast, reflecting the enormity of the disaster.

121

September 19, 1985 Earthquake in Mexico City

At 7.18 am local time (12.19 GMT) on September 19 1985 Mexico City, the most populous city in the world, with over 17 million inhabitants, was hit by an earthquake measuring 8.1 on the Richter scale.

Survivors have described it as being 'like the end of the world'. Buildings, many of them high-rise, swayed 'as if they were dancing' and many collapsed. Concrete and glass flew through the air. Some people stayed inside dodging their possessions as they crashed and tumbled about. Others ran into the streets down swaying staircases, hanging on to rails that moved, and avoiding plaster and other debris that fell from ceilings and walls.

In the streets they held on to trees as the ground shook under them. Clouds of dust rose from collapsed buildings and there was a smell of gas from fractured mains. All lights went out as power lines were severed; high tension cables were seen to snap and fall into the street. Without power, the underground system failed, and hundreds were stranded for several hours. National and international telephone and telex links were cut, with a fire at the central communications tower. Other buildings caught fire too and soon a thick pall of smoke and dust covered the area.

Crowds gathered on the streets. Many searched for relatives and friends and there was immediate concern for survivors trapped in the rubble whose cries for help could be heard. As soon as the shock waves stopped, thousands of people began a spontaneous civilian rescue operation. Where machines were not available, they used shovels or whatever they could find; if nothing was available, they dug with bare hands through the twisted metal and shattered masonry. They listened for sounds of life under the debris, often calling for quiet so that they could hear even the faintest noise. Sometimes rescuers would go to a specific address in answer to a plea broadcast over television or radio giving details of help and equipment required. They often worked under threat to their own lives from the further collapse of damaged buildings.

The second shock came on the evening of the 20th and, although weaker and less devastating than the first, it was still massive and no less terrifying. Some said they found it even more frightening because they did not think they would be so lucky as to escape twice.

Civilians continued to play a major role in the rescue operations throughout the crisis, showing impressive solidarity and discipline. President Miguel de la Madrid ordered three days of national mourning but the Mexican government was slow in starting a co-ordinated rescue operation. It declared a state of emergency and Mexico City a disaster zone. The military were called in to help but not at first given a specific role or instructions. They cordoned off areas and spent considerable time looking out for looters. The government initially refused international help, both technical and financial, but later it accepted, and aid poured in from all over the world. Vital rescue equipment, such as cutting tools and thermal image cameras to detect survivors by their body warmth, were flown in. So too were medical supplies and doctors, demolition experts and German shepherd dogs to help search for survivors and bodies. Professional rescue teams from five countries joined the Mexicans to work round the clock at their daunting task.

The supreme efforts of the rescuers were not in vain. For more than a week they continued to find and save people still alive in the ruins. Among the damaged buildings were several of the city's hospitals, including the Juarez. Here, seven days after the first shock, a woman patient and a tiny premature baby were brought out alive. Later that day a nurse, Angela Mendez, was also rescued. Her calls for help had been heard some 24 hours earlier but a 40-foot (12m) tunnel had to be dug to reach her. This was done by a team of Miami firemen and Mexican miners, working with hammers and chisels.

New-born babies were also rescued alive from other devastated hospitals – over 60 up to a period of more than a week after the first shock. Their survival captured interest and imagination worldwide. It has been explained as being due to their lack of psychological stress which consumes so much vital energy in those aware of their plight. Dehydration was their main problem. The last two survivors reported taken from the rubble were two more babies.

At this point, ten days after the first earth-

Right: helpers pulling a victim out of the rubble after the devastation of the earthquake. Such work went on for more than ten days.

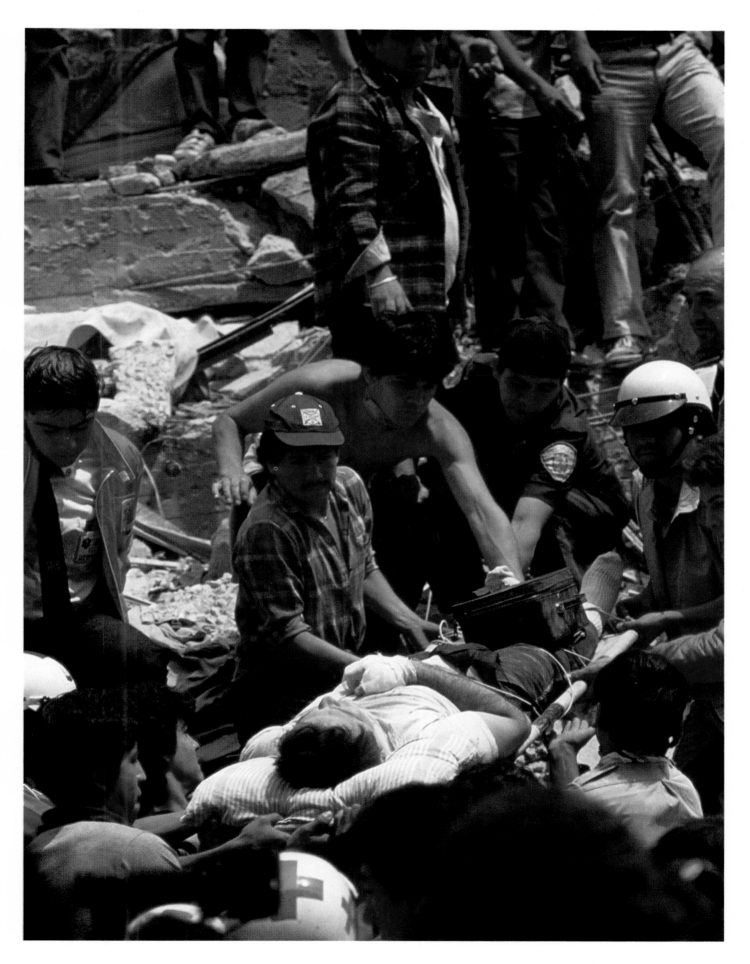

quake, hopes of finding more survivors were fading. The risks to the health of the rescue workers and other inhabitants of the city were increasing each day from the thousands of bodies still buried in the ruined buildings. All relief workers wore clinical face masks, and medical teams were out in the street injecting people against typhoid and tetanus. No survivors were found on the 29th and the Health Ministry now ordered the fumigation of all collapsed buildings, and demolition teams with heavy equipment and dynamite moved in to begin clearing away the ruins.

Again because of fears of an epidemic, and also because of the sheer numbers involved, bodies that had been recovered were buried in huge mass graves. Identification was an extremely difficult problem. Appeals were broadcast on radio and television for relatives or friends to come forward to identify bodies. But after a certain time, bodies were photographed and buried unidentified because of the disease risk. On the other side of this anguish were those who spent weeks looking for relatives who were missing and simply could not be traced, alive or dead. The broadcasting companies were again very helpful in trying to put people in contact with each other by issuing personal details when requested.

The final death toll will never be known. Official and unofficial estimates vary widely. The Mexican government, which minimized figures throughout, gave a total of about 5000 and the Economic Commission for Latin America, 7000 dead and some 30,000 injured. Unofficial figures from some government members, and rescue workers who were actually on the scene, put the figure at well above 10,000 and probably nearer 20,000 dead. Experts have also pointed out that if the shock had been an hour or so later offices and schools in the worst-hit area would have been fully occupied and the toll very much higher.

As it was, the problem in human and material terms was daunting. Dangerous buildings had been evacuated by order of the authorities, while as many as 250,000 people had evacuated their homes from choice to live in the streets, in tents or makeshift shelters, rather than in any building. There they joined those whose homes had been destroyed, for whom centres were being organized. Over 1 million people were without running water. In terms of material damage, insurance companies, for example, expected claims on over 7000 buildings. Some estimates said that over one-third of all buildings had sustained some damaged, and other experts suggested that the foundations of most were affected. Rebuilding alone was expected to cost from $2 billion upwards.

Below: a family placing flowers on the grave of a relative – for many victims, however, mass graves (foreground) were the only solution to problems of identification and the need for quick burial.

On September 28 a cabinet meeting, presided over by President Miguel de la Madrid, discussed assistance for the hundreds of thousands of people affected and began to work out a programme for the reconstruction of the city. The state of emergency was over and rehabilitation was to get under way.

The greatest devastation was relatively localized in the city centre. It included the historic area known as the Zocala which is at the hub of the city's daily life. The Zocala has many fine examples of Spanish colonial architecture, including the Catedral Metropolitana, as well as several important government buildings. The main business district is in this central locality, as is the city's tourist centre with hundreds of hotels and restaurants. It is a residential area too, with many apartment blocks and schools, as well as several of the city's main hospitals.

Along the Paseo de la Reforma, the city's main office and hotel thoroughfare, buildings had collapsed onto the pavement. Near the National Palace, an eight-storey office and apartment block collapsed into a two-storey heap with the roof still complete on the top. In the central area alone 177 buildings collapsed completely and 81 partially. Other areas which suffered badly include the Tlateloco district to the east of the Zocala, and the area to the south round the National Medical Centre, which was itself damaged.

However, the greater part of the vast, sprawling city was not visibly affected by the earthquake. Although one engineer described the centre as shaking 'like a bowl of jelly', in the suburbs a few miles away the tremors were hardly noticeable. The question was raised as to why one part was damaged and not another and, more particularly, why one building and not its neighbours.

Above: *thousands of people lost relatives in the earthquake – but the tragedy would have been far greater if it had happened an hour or so later.*

Above: the high-rise concrete buildings were the worst hit in the city, their deep foundations making them more unsafe than lower constructions as they picked up more of the vibrations.

Mexico has an advanced building code for earthquake-resistant design, yet many of the buildings which collapsed were modern and apparently built in conformity with the code. Some of them were found to be victims of corruption in the building trade and lack of official enforcement of the regulations. These corrupt practices came under sharp attack after the disaster, and a commission was set up to look into cases of non-compliance with the building code. It was also to study the code itself in the light of the type of buildings affected and the extent of damage to them. In most cases, however, it was found to be the earthquake alone, with its unprecedented severity, which was mainly responsible for the damage.

Mexico City, especially the original, central area, is built on a dried-up lake bed. The ground is soft clay on the top with harder layers underneath. Experts believe that the clay subsoil of the soft lake-bed amplified the shock waves and

thus the ground motion. Amplification may have been up to five times that of outlying districts with different soil foundations. Further, a coincidence in the resonant frequency of the clay and of buildings about 10 storeys high, particularly those in the centre of the city with deep foundations, caused them to shake more violently and for longer, and thus to suffer the worst damage. Among buildings of the most vulnerable height were the Juarez Hospital, which was 12 storeys high, and the Nuevo-Leon building, 13 storeys, part of a housing complex in the eastern suburbs of Tlateloco. Most of the people who died were in hospitals or housing blocks. It is thought that as many as 1000 died in each of the two mentioned. Taller buildings with longer vibration periods and shallow foundations shook less. The old Spanish colonial stone buildings, and other later ones of brick, also survived better than the many modern high-rise concrete and steel structures.

This combination of circumstances, then, caused Mexico City to suffer uniquely and at long distance. For the epicentre of the earthquake was some 250 miles (400km) away, off the west coast of Mexico, under the Pacific Ocean near Playa Acul. Other parts of the country suffered loss of life and damage but with nothing like the same intensity. The four coastal states of Michoacán, Jalisco, Colima and Guerrero were the worst hit, and buildings of all kinds were damaged. Destruction was widespread but sporadic. In Atentique, in Jalisco, part of a mountain slid away, killing the farm people in the valley below on their way to work. At Acapulco, the popular foreign tourist resort on the west coast and so not so far from the epicentre, there was only light damage and no casualties. The quakes affected a 310,000 square mile (2,080,000 sq km) zone. At sea several ships, mainly trawlers, sank near the epicentre and one trawler which survived described a 'boiling sea' with waves 70ft (21m) high. The shocks were felt as far north as Houston, Texas, 745 miles (1200km) away, and south in Guatemala City, 621 miles (1000km) away.

The earthquake highlighted and intensified the problems of Mexico, particularly those of its capital. Its considerable cost could not but add to the country's already critical financial situation, in spite of special aid and loans, including emergency assistance from the International Monetary Fund. It put new strains and demands on the existing vast housing shortage in Mexico City and drew attention to the government's failure to carry out its decentralization policy. Building problems were increased by the need for a major reappraisal of practices in this earthquake zone. The area flattened in 1985 was almost the same as that destroyed in an earthquake in 1957 in spite of the advanced building code, so this was an urgent issue if yet another, similar disaster was to be avoided.

Below: tents became home for the thousands of families displaced by the earthquake while the slow, arduous process of reclaiming the city began.

January 28, 1986
Space Shuttle
Challenger

In the United States, the National Aeronautics and Space Administration (NASA) designated 1986 the 'Year for Space Science'. It was the 25th anniversary of manned space flight, and as many as 15 space shuttle flights were planned for the year. During the 25 years Americans had gone into space and returned safely over 50 times. There was beginning to be a feeling of the commonplace, of everyday routine about it all, especially about the shuttle. First launched in 1981, it was a reusable, workaday sort of vehicle, its orbiter coming and going, much like an aeroplane. So on the occasion of the launch into space of the 25th shuttle mission, less people were watching than in the past; the three major US television networks were not even broadcasting it live. The disaster which occurred changed everything.

Mission 51-L, space shuttle Challenger, had experienced problems before it was finally launched on January 28. After three previous postponements, only the day before the astronauts had been strapped into their seats when the launch was called off again because of a broken handle on a hatch and then delayed further because of high winds. In addition, that night the temperature dropped and severe cold, unusual in Florida, deposited thick ice on the launch pad. So on the morning of the 28th, ground crew were at the pad removing icicles.

Nevertheless, the launch went ahead as planned. At 11.38 am, Challenger rose into a clear blue sky at Cape Canaveral in what appeared to be another perfect lift-off. Yet within 75 seconds the vehicle was engulfed in a fireball, had disintegrated and was falling back to Earth in pieces. The seven astronauts on board had lost their lives.

The immediate reaction of those watching was one of stunned disbelief. In mission control the public affairs officer, Steve Nesbitt, was not watching the pictures on the monitor but looking at his data consoles. So he continued to give flight information as if all were normal, seconds after others had seen the shuttle fall apart in a ball of fire. Then, as cameras tracked falling debris, he said 'Obviously a major malfunction' and finally '. . . the vehicle has exploded'. As reality began to register, horror and grief took over. The news spread fast. Television channels abandoned regular programmes to show brief videotapes of the launch over and over again. Congress adjourned and normal life across the United States was disrupted. President Reagan postponed his 'State of the Union' address, due that evening, and went on television to speak about the disaster instead.

Before the accident little interest had been taken in the seven astronauts, with one exception. This was Sharon Christa McAuliffe, the first 'ordinary' private citizen (two Congressmen had been before) to go on a shuttle flight. She was a schoolteacher from New Hampshire who had won her place through a national screening begun in 1984. The idea was

Previous page:
Challenger's final liftoff, which should have been just another routine launch, was soon to turn into a horrific tragedy.
Right: *the moment, eventually watched by millions worldwide, when the Challenger exploded in a ball of fire and the seven crew members on board lost their lives.*

that she should conduct at least two televised lessons from space and on her return tour the United States lecturing students about her trip and so stimulate interest in high-tech careers.

The others members of the crew were the flight commander, Francis 'Dick' Scobee; the pilot, Michael Smith; mission specialists Judith Resnik, Ellison Onizuka and Ronald McNair, and Hughes Aircraft engineer Gregory Jarvis. It has been noted that they were a crew who 'represented all Americans' – male and female, black and white, Protestant, Catholic and Jewish. A primary goal of their mission was to launch TDRS–B, a communications satellite, the second part of a badly-needed continuous-link system between ground stations and orbiting spacecraft.

Christa McAuliffe's death was made even more poignant by the fact that many of those who were watching the launch as it happened were doing so simply because she, an ordinary teacher with whom they could identify, was on board. The audience naturally included many schoolchildren, among them her own class who had presented her with an apple as she climbed aboard the shuttle. President Reagan addressed them directly as he paid tribute to Challenger's crew in his televised speech that evening when he said 'I know it's hard to understand that sometimes painful things like this happen. It's all part of the process of exploration and discovery . . . The future doesn't belong to the fainthearted, it belongs to the brave.'

Immediate, intensive investigations into the causes of the accident were undertaken by NASA and by a commission appointed by President Reagan. The Presidential Commission, headed by former secretary of state William Rogers, was to be independent 'to secure an impartial review'. Its members included scientists, engineers and astronauts. Their aim was to reconstruct as fully as possible what happened. They were assisted in this by the workers at NASA who were profoundly shocked by what had happened to their colleagues. It was a particular grief to them that, in spite of many emergency contingency plans, in the event they had been able to do nothing at all because of the accident's instant finality. They threw themselves into the painstaking study of every detail of the launch to understand what had happened and to prevent it ever happening again. Together with and in support of the presidential commission, they spent weeks collecting data, looking at thousands of photographs, and piecing together all the evidence available.

The physical evidence for the investigations was retrieved from the Atlantic Ocean where debris rained down for more than an hour after the shuttle disintegrated. A pall of smoke over the water marked the area where most of it fell. A fleet of recovery vessels began an intensive search and salvage operation to find the crew and retrieve the wreckage. Sonar surveys were made to search the seabed. Immediately after the break-up the forward section of the shuttle orbiter, containing the crew cabin, was seen to be still relatively intact and to coast on upwards before falling back to Earth. But the crew were not found. The only human remains among the tons of debris finally collected were a small piece of bone and body tissue.

The two solid fuel rocket boosters which flanked the shuttle survived the fireball, separated prematurely and continued flying. Then they began to career out of control and about 30 seconds later were detonated by mission control because they were dangerously near populated areas of the Florida coastline. Although pieces of them were retrieved in the debris, in a very real sense NASA was here being forced unwittingly to destroy a major part of the evidence. For the physical cause of the accident was quickly pinpointed as being in one of the booster rockets.

The first sign that something had gone wrong was eight puffs of dark grey smoke from the base of the right-hand booster rocket while Challenger was still on the launch pad. This was not visible to most of those watching the launch because it was on the side of the craft away from most cameras, but it showed up later on a film being made for NASA to the north of Cape Canaveral. Nor were mission control or the shuttle crew aware of any problem because nothing showed on the instruments or in the computer data from the thousands of sensors on both the orbiter and the rocket.

The exact location of the smoke was at a joint between the lower two sections of the four-section cylindrical booster rocket. The source of the smoke was the rubber O-rings which were designed to seal the joints between the sections of the booster. There were two .27-inch (.71cm) thick rings in each seal, one to back up if the first failed, their efficiency crucial to the booster rockets and the safety of the whole shuttle. The pressure of the burning fuel should have seated the rings in the gap between the sections. In Challenger's case, however, the very low temperatures before the launch had made the rubber of the O-rings stiff and brittle, and with reduced resilience they did not regain their shape to fill and reseal the gap, which widened when the rockets were fired.

So hot gases from the burning fuel escaped past the rings, burning the rubber. A congealed mass of burned rubber and aluminium oxides in the joint then actually closed the gap. If this had held for about two minutes when the booster rockets were to be jettisoned the shuttle might have survived. However, about 40 seconds into the flight a new factor came into play which dealt the final blow to Challenger's chances. For it encountered the strongest wind shear a shuttle had ever experienced. An estimated 30 seconds of buffeting dislodged whatever protection the burned rubber mass provided as the wind bent and flexed the rocket, stressing its joints.

Left: National Transportation Safety Board investigator John White examining the Challenger's right solid rocket booster nose cone for clues to explain the explosion.
Below: a portion of Challenger's payload door salvaged off the coast of Florida; much debris fell into the Atlantic, but human remains were virtually non-existent.

A flame first broke through the joint at 58 seconds. At first relatively small, about 8 feet (2.4m) long, it quickly grew to some 40 feet (12m). This was still not visible to most of those watching. The flame acted like a blowtorch, burning its way into the side of the shuttle's huge main-engine fuel tank, which contained liquid hydrogen and liquid oxygen, at the same time cutting through one of the three struts attaching the booster rocket to the tank. It burned like this for about 14 seconds. It was now visible on television as a very faint 'orange glow' below the fuel tank. Then at 72.2 seconds the strut gave way, the rocket pivoted and its nose was forced through the top of the tank. The tank collapsed and exploded as the liquid hydrogen and oxygen ignited. The shuttle fell apart, the boosters veering away from the orbiter which was itself broken into several sections. Smoke poured out of the lighted mass and debris began to fall back to Earth, 73 seconds after lift-off and about 47,000 feet (14,240m) up.

This detail of the events of the accident was pieced together by the NASA enquiry and the Presidential Commission after the event. At the time everything appeared to be normal from lift-off. Mission control at Houston gave the expected call 'Challenger, go at throttle up'. At 68 seconds after the launch, Commander Dick Scobee replied 'Roger go at throttle up'. Within a few seconds came the explosion. Tapes salvaged from the debris revealed that the instant before the break-up the pilot, Michael Smith, said 'Uh-oh'. Nothing else was heard and it is not known how or when the crew died. It is thought they may have survived the break-up but lost consciousness within seconds with the loss of cabin pressure since they did not wear pressure suits.

The report of the Presidential Investigating Committee, in June 1986, not only dealt with the immediate physical causes of the accident but also with the underlying faults which allowed it to happen. The accident, it considered, was 'rooted in history' and had been 'avoidable'. It described NASA management as 'lackadaisical' and its decision to launch Challenger as 'flawed'. Engineers at Morton-Thiokol, the company that built the rockets, had repeatedly warned over a period of three years about the safety of the O-ring seals and design problems of the booster joints, but they had gone unheeded by their superiors. Right up to the last minute they had tried to get NASA to call off the launch, because they considered the subzero temperatures a threat to the O-rings. They had been overruled by management. 'Even the most cursory examination', the report said, 'should

have indicated that a serious and potentially distastrous situation was developing in all solid rocket booster joints.' It blamed NASA for 'overreaching' itself, for breaking safety rules and using poorly-designed critical equipment, constantly skirting disaster in its overwhelming desire to keep the shuttle programme on schedule. This pressure had kept the shuttle flying in a dangerous condition. NASA's response was to improve communications between managers and engineers and to introduce a new safety office.

The accident was a serious blow to the whole American space programme. The shuttle was relied on as the main launch system and primary means of space transport for all kinds of payload. NASA was extremely demoralized as 1986 turned into the worst year in space for the United States. In August, however, President Reagan ordered construction of a new fourth shuttle, Discovery, to replace Challenger, with redesigned booster rockets and incorporating safety improvements as recommended by the accident report. This was to be launched in August 1988. Also, as a major policy change for NASA, shuttles would no longer be used to launch commercial satellites but would concentrate on scientific research and military payloads. However, a space station was to be built by 1994 using manned shuttle flights, and the sense of national loss at the Challenger disaster regnerated interest in the space programme and put it high on the political agenda. Christa McAuliffe's message to the schoolchildren of America that 'the new frontier is out in space' was taken up by the whole nation.

Below: *The official pre-flight photograph of the crew of Challenger: (back row) Ellison Onizuka, Christa McAuliffe, Gregory Jarvis, Judith Resnik; (front row) pilot Michael Smith, flight commander Dick Scobee, Ronald McNair.*

April 26, 1986
Explosion
at Chernobyl

The disaster at Chernobyl nuclear power station in April 1986 was the world's worst nuclear accident. The plant, situated 80 miles (130 km) north of Kiev in the Ukraine, is one of the largest nuclear complexes in the Soviet Union.

The complex sequence of events which led to the disaster was finally pieced together by the Soviet authorities. In a report published in August 1986 they gave a frank account of the accident, its local effects and the measures taken to deal with it. A week after publication, delegates from 45 countries met at the International Atomic Energy Agency (IAEA) headquarters in Vienna to discuss its causes and the aftermath.

The cause of the accident was given as a combination of human error and defects in the design of the reactor. The 'human error' involved was largely the deliberate violation of operating rules and disregard of safety procedures even to the point of overriding the plant's built-in protection systems.

It emerged that the staff concerned were conducting an unauthorised experiment to discover how long a steam turbine would continue to freewheel, and how much electricity it would generate while doing so, when its normal supply of steam from the reactor was shut off. The report did not give the purpose of the experiment, but experts have suggested it may have been to test the turbine's ability to produce enough electricity to compensate for any inadequacy in emergency power supply, particularly that for operating the coolant circulation pumps. For

this reason the reactor was not shut down during the experiment.

The type of reactor involved was an RBMK–1000, a design unique to the Soviet Union. It has a graphite core penetrated by over 1500 cylindrical fuel-channels. Water boils within the core itself to generate the steam to drive the turbines. It is water-cooled using ordinary water.

Preparation for the experiment began in the early hours of April 25 when operation of reactor No 4 was reduced to 50 per cent of its full power. Later that day the emergency core-cooling system was disconnected and power level further reduced. By 1am on April 26 it was as low as 7 per cent and all the reactor's safety features had been turned off. Any subsequent emergency reactor protector systems were blocked off as they occurred.

At 1.23am (2100 April 25 GMT) preparations were completed and steam to the turbine from the reactor was shut off. The turbine slowed down, then the circulation pumps slowed down and the flow of coolant to the reactor decreased. There was an immediate sharp rise in temperature in the reactor and a rapid increase in power production from 7 per cent to 50 per cent. The supervisor, realizing the danger, at once ordered the insertion of control rods to shut the reactor down, but it was already too overheated and the rods would not go in fully. The reactor and the situation were bu now out of control.

The swift power surge caused the fuel ele-

Previous page: the nuclear power plant at Chernobyl after the explosion.
Above: an aerial view of the plant two weeks after the explosion; the site of the accident is arrowed.
Right: the plant at Chernobyl in August 1986, by which time international safeguards had been implemented as a result of the incident.

136

ments to fragment and come into contact with the cooling water which immediately turned to steam. The rise in power was already generating vast quantities of steam in the reactor and this further huge build-up of pressure caused a massive explosion. It blew the protective slab off the top of the reactor vessel and the roof off the building, together with the refuelling hall which surmounted the reactor. There was no contain-

ment building. Another explosion and a fire followed within seconds, as water and steam reacted with the hot graphite in the reactor core to produce carbon monoxide and hydrogen which, with the reactor open to the air, ignited and burned out of control. Fortunately, the reator itself shut down and there was no chain reaction.

The amount of radioactive material released

Right: a diagram showing the resulting levels of radiation up to 1500 miles from Chernobyl, and the effects of radiation sickness.

Right: infra-red satellite pictures taken over Chernobyl (arrowed) immediately before and after the explosion, showing the prevailing weather conditions.

was unprecedentedly large. Sizeable lumps of radioactive fuel were blasted out of the reactor, landing on surrounding buildings where they started fires or on the ground within about half a mile (1km) of the plant. In addition, the sheer force of the explosion sent a huge plume of many tons of radioactive dust and gas high into the atmosphere. The radioactive materials included iodine-131 and caesium-137, both of which are readily absorbed by living tissue. The plume or 'cloud', as it became known, was initially carried on the wind high above the Soviet Union towards Finland and Sweden where some of it came down.

On April 28, technicians at Forsmark in Sweden, some 900 miles (1500km) from Chernobyl, detected abnormally high levels of radiation. There was confusion about its source at first but later the Soviet Union announced that there had been an accident and described its nature and location. It asked Swedish experts for help with a 'graphite fire', and on April 30 approached the IAEA in Vienna for advice. This resulted in a team from the Agency, including the director, Hans Blick, going to the Soviet Union to investigate the situation and give help where possible.

Meanwhile, at Chernobyl, strenuous efforts were continuing to put out the fire in the devastated reactor and to stop the release of radioactive material. Great heroism was displayed by the firefighters, mostly power-station workers

and firemen, who risked their lives as they fought to prevent fire from spreading to the other three reactors. Two firemen were killed and others, together with Chernobyl workers at the blaze, were among those who died later in hospital.

Considerable scientific ingenuity was required to bring the situation under control. Water could not be used on the burning graphite as it would create clouds of radioactive steam. It had to be extinguished by starving it of oxygen. So 5000 tons of lead, boron, dolomite, clay and sand were dropped from helicopters on to the top of the reactor. This may have put the graphite fire out but heat was still being generated by radioactive decay at the core and by the ninth day after the accident the release of radioactivity was nearly three-quarters the amount on the day of the explosion. To reduce it and prevent a future recurrence of fire, the vault under the reactor was filled with nitrogen.

Finally, the ruined reactor was encased in a giant sarcophagus: a thick, reinforced concrete 'box' with a three-layer concrete slab underneath to prevent contamination of ground water. When this was complete radioactive emissions were at last stopped.

Considering the scale of the accident, casualty figures in the immediate vicinity of Chernobyl were very low. Reasons for this include the fact that it happened at night when people were indoors and that still weather conditions allowed

Above: measures to decontaminate the land surrounding the plant included spraying the ground from helicopters.

the radioactive plume from the explosion to rise high and be blown away, initially across sparsely-populated farmland and forest. No one off the Chernobyl site suffered acute radiation poisoning but thousands of people throughout the Ukraine were exposed to significant doses of radiation.

After an initial delay, due to lack of correct information about the severity of the accident, all the inhabitants within a 20 mile (30km) zone around Chernobyl were evacuated with great speed and efficiency. Some 135,000 people were transported in over 1000 buses to other areas where they were provided with housing. All evacuees were given iodine tablets to help prevent the build-up of radioactive iodine-131 in the thyroid gland. They were also screened for exposure to radiation and about 18,000 were referred for further tests. For 40 years at least, their health and that of everyone else exposed to radiation will be monitored at a special centre set up in Kiev.

Those injured at the site were also treated quickly and efficiently by a specialist medical team flown in from Moscow on the day of the accident. Some 300 patients were flown to Moscow for treatment in the first two days; over 200 were diagnosed as having acute radiation sickness. Six weeks later 24 had died and 80 were still in a serious condition. Of these casualties, all of those with acute radiation poisoning who died also had severe thermal burns. Later reports indicate that other deaths from radiation sickness alone also occurred, particularly among control room personnel. Bone marrow transplants were given to 13 but most died of other injuries before they had a chance to take. The death toll as an immediate result of the accident was given in August as 31. Estimates of possible long-term casualty rates in the Soviet Union vary considerably.

Controls on agricultural production and foodstuffs were introduced by the Soviet authorities. The immediate problem was from deposits of fallout on the leaves of crops consumed by animals or human beings. In the long term, contamination of the soil itself is the hazard, particularly by caesium-137 which has a half-life of 30 years., Some Soviet farmers may have contaminated fields for well over a decade.

Decontamination of the worst-affected area in the 20 mile (30km) zone around Chernobyl presented a continuous long-term task. It has involved excavating heavily contaminated soil and using special polymers to treat the buildings and ground around the reactor to help reduce the spread of radioactive dust. Frequent spraying with water is also used over a wide area to keep the dust at ground level. A number of monitoring stations have been set up and soil and water samples are regularly tested. The fall in levels of radioactivity has been encouraging. A new town, Zelyony Mys, was created for Chernobyl workers while Chernobyl itself was 'cleaned up'. Contamination of ground and surface water presented other problems, particularly because the area drains into the Dnieper River which flows into the Black Sea.

Further afield, the nuclear 'cloud' was carried on the winds throughout western and eastern Europe, as far south as Greece and north to the Arctic Circle. It reached the United States and possibly Japan. The amount that fell in each country varied with factors such as rainfall and the lie of the land over which it passed. People were naturally concerned, particularly because there were conflicting reports and opinions as to whether there was any real danger and what action should be taken.

Governments reacted in various ways. Most began more intensive measurement of radioactivity in the air and some in water and fresh foodstuffs too. Countermeasures taken depended on the level found and on permitted safety levels which varied widely. In Poland, for example, the government banned the sale of milk from grass-fed cows and iodine tablets were issued, while in France and Italy huge amounts of fresh vegetables were dumped or at least checked for radiation before sale. In Britain, nothing was done until June when a ban was imposed on sheep movement in Cumbria, North Wales and Scotland as radiation levels built up there. Experts tended to indicate that there was little immediate risk to people but that in coming decades an increase in deaths from cancers could be expected.

The Soviet Union modified its reactor design to deal with defects found as a result of the Chernobyl inquiry. It also said that safety lessons had been learned and implemented with the introduction of fail-safe procedures. In addition, operators were to be better trained and control systems better designed to eliminate the possibilities of future human error or deliberate interference.

In July 1987 six officials at Chernobyl were tried for causing the accident by carrying out unauthorized experiments. They included the power station's director, Viktor Bryukhanov, who was also accused of giving misinformation about the scale of the disaster and so delaying the evacuation of people in the area. Most countries discussed very seriously the safety of their own nuclear plants and whether they should continue with nuclear power. The majority of them decided to carry on with existing policies, but differences of opinion between those for and those against where sharpened and people's confidence in the safety of the nuclear power industry was severely shaken worldwide.

To help restore confidence and to try to avoid such a widespread disaster as Chernobyl in future, two international conventions were drawn up by the IAEA. Under these countries agreed to provide early notification and information about nuclear accidents, even at military installations, and to offer mutual assistance and cooperation when such an event was likely to have 'trans-boundary' effects as Chernobyl was the first to do.

Right: iodine solution being administered to a child in Warsaw to combat possible radiation poisoning.
Inset: liquid decontamination trucks helping to reduce the high levels of radiation.

NORTH SEA

Zeebrugge

BELGIUM

FRANCE

March 6, 1987
Herald of Free
Enterprise

A cryptic two-word phone message 'Zeebrugge Alarm' alerted the people of that Belgian port to a disaster on March 6, 1987. Immediately, a well-rehearsed crisis plan swung into action. Each person on receiving the message phoned one other and then left for their designated post. No questions were asked. Even the governor of West Flanders, Olivier Vanneste, who received the first call did not know what had happened as he drove to the appointed crisis centre. Within 15 minutes of that first call everyone was ready. By now they knew that the disaster had happened at sea.

At about 19.05 (18.05 GMT) the British car-ferry *Herald of Free Enterprise*, owned by Townsend Thoresen, had set sail from Zeebrugge a few minutes behind schedule, bound for Dover. There were over 600 people on board, including 80 crew, and about 120 vehicles. It was a cold, clear night and the sea was calm. The ship sailed towards the mouth of the harbour, gathering speed as it went. Suddenly, just outside the harbour, it began to list to port and within one minute it had capsized. It settled on a shallow sand bank, the only thing which prevented it from sinking completely.

For those on board it was an instant total nightmare as in a matter of seconds everything turned on its side, it went pitch dark and icy cold water began to rise rapidly around them.

During the first few seconds, as the ferry listed slightly, passengers though that it was just the sea getting a bit rough. Then they noticed water coming up past the windows on the port side and suddenly realized to their horror that it was going right over. As it did so some windows smashed and passengers near them were sucked out into the sea. People grabbed hold of anything fixed to stop themselves falling, as floors became walls and everything loose crashed down around them. Those who lost their grip were thrown down, in some cases almost the whole width of the boat. Then all the lights went out and water rose rapidly inside the vessel. Some managed to clamber up the furniture, using the seats like a climbing frame, trying to keep ahead of the water. Others were sucked into it.

There was mass panic as so many terrified human beings, in a dark confined space, followed the basic instinct of self-preservation and fought to escape. Some were injured in the sheer crush. As far as they knew the ship could still have been sinking. But amidst all this there was courage and bravery and many lives were saved by the action of others, sometimes at the risk, even the cost, of their own. Many who found a 'safe place' above the water pulled others up beside them. Children were passed from one adult to another and while they waited for help were comforted by strangers.

Crew members, whose emergency training had not prepared them for an accident involving a capsize, nevertheless played a major role in helping people to safety. They were among the

Left: the capsized Herald of Free Enterprise *on the day after the tragedy, held in place by rescue ships while the search for victims continued.*

Above: a helicopter winching survivors from the Herald while the rescue operation continued relentlessly.

first to climb out onto the exposed side of the ferry through smashed windows, and pulled others out using ropes, hosepipes, anything that would do the job. Ironically, the ferry had sophisticated emergency equipment, including escape chutes like those on aircraft, but nearly all of it was useless in this situation, being only usable when the ship was upright.

There were many heroic acts by passengers too. Stan Mason, who suffered spinal injuries, saved his baby daughter by carring her in his teeth as he climbed over tables and chairs. Andrew Parker, who is 6ft 3in (1.9m) tall, made his own body into a human bridge by stretching between two metal barriers across a gap filled with water. Some 20 terrified people, including his own wife and daughter, climbed over him to safety.

The intense cold of the water, given by har-

bour officials as 3 degrees Celsius, was a main enemy. A person would not normally be expected to survive in it for more than about 15 minutes. It was a race against time and, to those on board the *Herald of Free Enterprise*, the ordeal seemed endless.

In fact, the first help arrived at the stricken ferry only about a quarter of an hour after the capsize. The alarm was raised by the crew of a dredger, the *San Derus*, which was about a mile away and had seen the ferry tilt and its lights go out. The dredger moved as near as possible to the ferry and the crew lowered a dinghy and rescued the first 40 survivors. Several tugs and other small boats were soon on the scene. The tugs included the *Fighter* from Antwerp and the *Holland*, which stayed throughout the operation, plying in and out from Zeebrugge first with survivors and later with the bodies of victims.

The alarm call set in motion a full-scale air-sea rescue operation. As soon as it was received at Zeebrugge's naval base a NATO exercise there was cancelled and operation 'Harbour Rescue' began. The speed at which this operation was mounted, a flotilla of NATO boats being already in the area, saved precious time, and thus many lives, as survivors waited, soaking wet, inside the flooded vessel or out on the exposed hull. A Belgian Air Force helicopter was first on the scene followed by others from Holland, Germany and Britain, together with ships and divers. For four hours they were engaged ceaselessly in rescue and recovery operations. Some 46 service divers were working at one time, going down into the ferry to get survivors out and later to recover bodies. The ships searched the surrounding sea. The whole area was lit from above by helicopter searchlights.

As the survivors were taken off, some of the injured were winched into the helicopters on stretchers and flown directly to hospital. Others crowded into the small boats which surrounded the ferry and returned to the dock at Zeebrugge. Here they were met by the 'front line' of the remarkable 'Zeebrugge Alarm' crisis plan. Scores of waiting ambulances took more of the injured to hospital, while emergency dressing stations treated those with minor injuries at the dockside. All the survivors were immediately wrapped in blankets and those who could walk were put on waiting buses to take them to hotels, where they were given dry clothing and rooms for the night.

No one was actually on the quay for more than one minute, as a positive medical decision because of the low temperature. All were suffering from varying degrees of shock and exposure, and some were close to death from hypothermia.

Below: an aerial view of the Herald *showing the total extent of the capsize.*

In all 408 people survived the disaster, 189 died and four, including a baby, were unaccounted for. Because ferries do not have passenger lists, some people had the anguish of having to wait for weeks before they knew for certain that their missing relative or friend was among the dead. The delay was so long because conditions inside the hull were so dangerous, with falling debris and oil from vehicles, that there was no safe way for divers to recover all the bodies before the ship was pulled upright. This was done on April 7, a month after the accident. The ferry then had to be pumped out and was finally refloated on April 27. Only then was it certain that all the remaining bodies – 104 in all – had been recovered.

A full public inquiry into the causes of the accident began in London on the same day, April 27. From the day after the disaster, when the tide went down, it was clear that the water had got into the ship through the bow doors which were gaping wide open. The main question to be answered was how they came to be open. The inquiry was also asked to consider the design and safety margins of roll-on roll-off (ro-ro) ferries and to make recommendations where necessary.

There was much public concern about the safety of ro-ro ferries, particularly because of the speed of the capsize. The main debate was about their stability. It is the open vehicle-deck design, with an undivided deck stretching the whole length of the vessel close to the waterline, that makes them more vulnerable than conventional ships which are subdivided into watertight compartments at all levels. In the case of the *Herald* the open deck was about 430 feet (132m) long. This design is undoubtedly the most efficient and thus the most economic. Vehicles and freight roll on through doors at one end and off through doors at the other, making turnrounds in port as fast as possible. But there was speculation that passenger safety had been made secondary to these economic considerations.

In normal circumstances ro-ro ferries are watertight vessels if correct procedures are followed. They have a thick steel double-door system opened and closed by huge hydraulic rams. Any small amounts of water which might get onto the vehicle deck are expelled through flash drains and bulkhead channels, thus not building up in any one place. However, a sudden, largish inrush of seawater onto the vehicle deck, caused by a collision for example, makes the ferry vulnerable to capsizing and sinking very quickly because the lack of bulkheads allows the water to surge about freely, causing great instability. In 1982, another Townsend Thoresen ro-ro ferry, *European Gateway*, had capsized within a few minutes of being holed amidships in a collision.

Below: after the Herald *had been righted, the vehicles on board were salvaged and police were able to search through the mud for any remaining victims.*

On the question of the open doors it appeared to be not uncommon to keep both bow and stern doors open within the harbour at least, mainly to ventilate the ship and rid it of vehicle fumes. The doors were normally about 12 feet (3.5m) above the waterline in harbour, but even in a calm sea at full speed a big enough bow wave could be produced to reach this level. Further, in some ports, including Zeebrugge, the bow had to be lowered by filling ballast tanks so that the ramp could reach the upper vehicle-deck. This gave clearance of only about 9 feet (2.7m) above the water and the ballast tanks took about 30 minutes to empty. On the day of the disaster those of the *Herald* had been filled because of the very high tide.

On July 24 Mr Justice Sheen, the Admiralty judge heading the inquiry, published his report. As expected, the immediate cause of the accident was found to be the fact that the bow doors were open. As the ship got up speed and left the harbour it turned sharply to port and a large quantity of water entered the vehicle deck causing a 30 degree initial tilt, followed within seconds by a capsize of over 90 degrees. There was no mechanical malfunction of the doors; they had simply not been closed. For this and other 'errors of omission', the ship's master, David Lewry, its chief officer, Leslie Sabel and assistant boatswain, Mark Stanley, were held directly responsible. The certificates of competence of the first two were suspended.

However, the judged blamed the underlying cause of the tragedy on the management of Townsend Thoresen which he described as 'infected with the disease of sloppiness'. In particular he criticized their 'failure to give clear orders about the duties of the officers on the Zeebrugge run' and especially the lack of proper standing orders to cover the closure of doors. But they had committed no statutory offence because there was no law that the bow or stern doors had to be closed when the ship went to sea. There was considerable public feeling about the punishment of the crew members while the management went scot-free. The government announced that it would introduce legislation to make it a criminal offence in future.

The report also made many wide-ranging recommendations for higher safety standards. Some of these, as it acknowledged, ships' masters had been urging on the management for months, only to be met with 'staggering complacency'. They included fitting warning lights on the bridge to show bow and stern doors closed, installing closed-circuit television to monitor the vehicle deck from the bridge, and supplying watertight emergency lighting units. These suggestions were immediately implemented by the Department of Transport. Longer-term measures included research into the stability of roll-on roll-off vessels, particularly a feasibility study on the possible use of bulkheads on the vehicle deck. These would probably need be removable without increas-

ing turnround time so much that they made the ferries uneconomical to run. The government gave £1 million towards this study.

Passengers had also made suggestions for improving safety equipment in the light of their experiences. These included lockers containing ladders, harnesses, torches and axes, and also escape windows and grab handles. All emergency equipment and procedures needed to be reconsidered because they were designed for use only when the boat was upright.

Public confidence was certainly shaken. Public sympathy for the victims was shown in the millions of pounds contributed to a disaster relief fund and in memorial services, while no one had enough praise for the rescue services, particularly those of Zeebrugge itself. Later in the year, inquest juries recorded verdicts of unlawful killing on 187 of the victims. Ship design, commented one naval architect, is always a compromise between safety and the ability of the vessel to perform economically. The balance seemed to have slipped in favour of economics. It is to be hoped that the disaster may have provoked a response which will make ferry travel safer for the millions of people who use these ships every year.

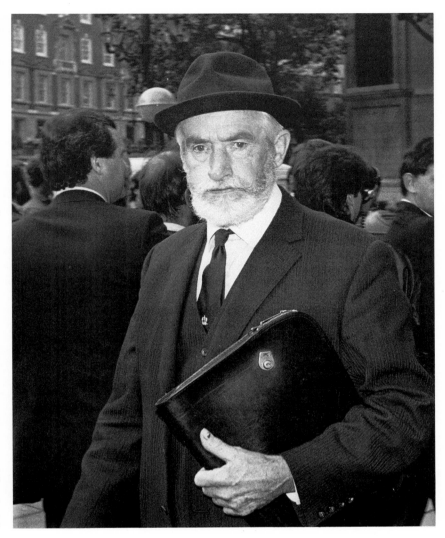

Above: Oliver Elson, captain of the Herald's *sister ship,* Spirit of Free Enterprise, *arriving at the High Court in London to hear the findings of the enquiry led by Mr Justice Sheen.*

November 18, 1987
Fire
at King's Cross

King's Cross

TICKET

Perhaps the most disturbing aspects of the disastrous fire at King's Cross Underground station in November 1987, excluding the loss of life and injuries sustained, were the terrifying speed at which it suddenly spread and the intense heat it generated. No one directly in its path stood a chance. In the accounts of survivors, time is measured in seconds and distances in yards. People who had just walked past a 'few puffs of smoke' suddenly had to run for their lives from a raging inferno which enveloped them in dense black smoke.

King's Cross, in central London, is one of the biggest intersections on the Underground system, serving five lines. It is a maze of tunnels, escalators, passageways, stairwells and platforms on several different levels. The booking hall concourse, where the main fire was, is itself underground.

At about 7.15pm on November 18, just after the evening rush hour, smoke was seen coming from a point about a third of the way down the number 4 escalator linking the booking hall to the Piccadilly line platforms. Some 15 minutes later a passenger noticed small flames on the escalator and it was then stopped. At 7.36 the fire brigade was called. The fire appeared to be quite small and a member of staff tried to put it out with an extinguisher. The fire brigade arrived at 7.46 and the first fire crews went down into the Underground without breathing apparatus in the belief that they would be dealing with a small fire. Indeed, one fireman described it as being the size of a burning cardboard box at this time.

The fire officer in charge, Colin Townsley, sent his men back up for breathing apparatus and a single hose to deal with the fire. He alone stayed underground to assess the situation and to direct passengers to safety. Exactly what happened next is still not clear but in a matter of a few seconds fire enveloped the whole booking hall in a totally unpredictable way. The heat was intense and thick black smoke engulfed everything. The most likely explanation is that there was a 'flashover' from the top of the burning escalator to the booking hall. This is characterized by a 'whooshing' noise, which survivors have said they heard, and a searing wall of flame moving faster than anyone can run.

Many people were trapped in the booking hall, unable to see the exits and overcome by the heat and smoke. One survivor described crawling along under a 'sheet of fire'. Others spoke of the sheer impossibility of reaching people only yards from safety. They shouted back down stairways and tunnels to people they knew were just behind them before the fire suddenly erupted, trying to guide and encourage them to the exits, but some of them just could not make it. Smoke was pouring out and those outside felt a horrifying sense of helplessness.

The firemen, now wearing breathing apparatus, went back down at great risk to their own lives into the almost totally unbearable heat to rescue survivors and fight the fire. Despite the conditions they managed to drag a number of people clear. Over 150 firemen and 30 appliances became involved in dealing with what had become a major incident. It was not until 9.48 that the message 'Fire surrounded' was heard, meaning it was at last under control, and it was nearly 5 am before the brigade could finally report that all persons were accounted for underground.

They were continuously hampered by the appalling heat and dense smoke and by falling debris. Tiles crashed from walls and ceiling, and concrete cracked as the heat built up in it. They had to keep close to the ground as they tackled the flames. Many of them were overcome by heat exhaustion but often after a rest above ground they returned to the scene. Some needed hospital treatment and one, Station Officer Townsley, lost his life. He was a very experienced fireman, yet even he must have been taken unawares by this fire. He could have saved himself by waiting to put on breathing apparatus but his immediate reaction was to help those around him. His colleagues found him unconscious about 25 yards (28m) from safety next to a passenger he was trying to rescue. He died later in hospital of smoke inhalation.

There were 31 deaths in all, including three members of one family, and several people had very serious injuries. The injured were taken to nearby hospitals along streets closed to all but emergency vehicles. Specialist teams of surgeons were called in to treat them. The worst affected were suffering from deep burns and lung problems caused by inhaling smoke. Plastic surgeons said that some of the injured had the most severe flash burns they had ever seen. These burns, caused by very high temperatures, were mainly on hands and faces. Stephen Hanson, a constable in the transport police who was injured, described his hands as having 'melted' in the heat.

Police, particularly the transport police, played an active role in trying to get passengers to safety, several of them being injured in the attempt. Both the fire brigade and the police dealt with the situation at King's Cross mainly on the basis of lessons learnt at the Oxford Circus Underground fire in 1984 when getting people to the surface as quickly as possible was the priority. It is also the natural and logical reaction when trapped undergound to go up and out. In the event, because of the location of the seat of this fire and its unusual nature, this was not the best course of action for those below the booking-hall level, although no one could have known that at the time.

The main escape route from this fire was, with hindsight, the trains. However, again based on previous experience, these were told not to stop at King's Cross so that people could not get off there. They were kept running to avoid those on board being trapped in smoke-filled tunnels. Ventilation in the London Underground depends on the movement of trains, and although there is the suggestion that the current of air may have fanned the flames, it almost certainly helped to push the fire away from the lower areas where most of the people were. At the time none of this was any consolation to those trapped at platform level with their escape route cut off.

There was a great deal of confusion from the time the fire was first reported. Although it was then quite small, there was obviously some smoke and some passengers began to be evacuated via the the booking hall. However, others were still being allowed into the station and right down to platform level even after the fire brigade arrived. The trains were still stopping at this time and people were getting off. Some, on smelling the burning, tried to get back on again, but those who were waiting had filled the train and they were left behind. An announcement said there was no cause for alarm as it was 'only a small litter fire'. Passengers being directed upwards were told to use the Victoria line escalator, the top of which was near the seat of the fire, but, because of its apparently minor

nature, this seemed to present no danger. Then the flashover occurred and the situation changed totally in the booking hall, but those below it did not know this and passengers went on going up.

Some of these met the full force of the flashover and were among those who died or were very severely burned. Others, who were already further across the concourse, suffered from the effects of smoke and intense heat and some of them were also among the dead. Some survivors have described how as the escalator rose they felt the heat increase and they raced back down again as the smoke thickened, only to find that the trains were no longer stopping. It was many hours before the emergency services were finally satisfied that everyone trapped underground was accounted for.

In one incident, police tried to get a badly burned man out via the Midland City exit but they were hampered by two locked gates. It took 20 minutes to get the two people needed to open them. This exit, a long subway away from the main concourse, could (and should) have been a way out for many others much earlier.

Below: *the head of the escalators where the fire began, showing the extent of the damage.*
Inset: *a plan of King's Cross underground station showing the location of the fire.*

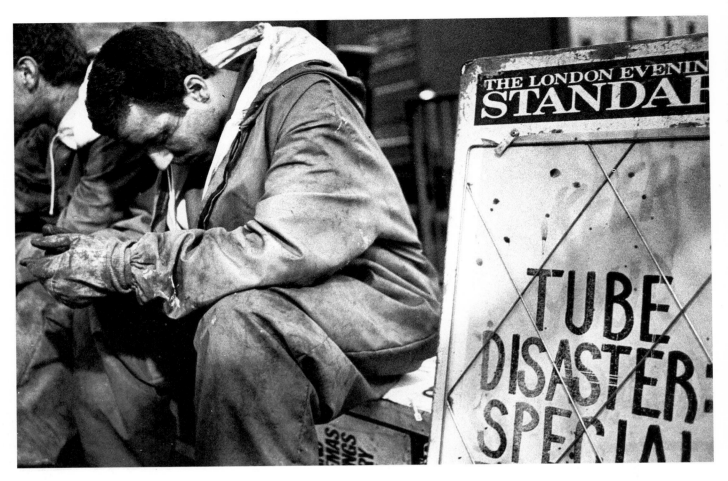

Above: nearly 24 hours after the fire, a worker takes a necessary rest outside the station before resuming the salvage operation.

A public enquiry into the causes of the accident and lessons to be learned from it was set up under Desmond Fennell, QC, assisted by four assessors. Forensic scientists and investigators for London Regional Transport (LRT), the police and fire services sifted through the debris and examined other evidence and their findings were made available to the inquiry. One of the most difficult questions it faced was why the fire developed so rapidly.

Experts agreed that the fire had begun in a mixture of grease and dirt on the wheel track of the number 4 escalator. It was probably ignited by a lighted match thrown away by a smoker, which may have fallen through a gap between the escalator tread and the skirting board at the edge. Smoking was banned in most of the Underground but people often lit or discarded cigarettes on escalators when on their way in or out. The fire on the grease, of which there was about a third of a ton, could have burned for some time unseen and so built up heat. When the fire brigade was called the flames appeared to be under 1 inch (2cm) long, but expert witnesses from the Health and Safety Executive said that only the tips of the flames were visible and the whole flame was by then about 3 feet (1m) long, the rest being under the escalator treads. The primary seat of the fire was about halfway down the 130-foot (40m) escalator, the apparent seat, about a third of the way down, being only secondary.

The fire spread from the grease to the plywood skirting boards and side panels of the escalator and then to the wood of the stairs. It is at this point that expert opinion divides, specifically about what caused the sudden speeding up in the spread of the fire, and in particular what role, if any, was played in this by the paint on the ceiling of the escalator shaft. The Health and Safety Executive, backed by other experts, blamed the speed of the burning solely on the wood of the escalator. They used a computer simulation and a model of the fire and maintained that the flames had spread mainly at low level, in the trough of the escalator, up the incline of the shaft and so the ceiling of the shaft stayed relatively cool. The flames which first reached the booking hall were then from the burning wood of the escalator and not the paint on the ceiling.

London Regional Transport's theories of the cause of the sudden spread of the fire all blamed the paint on the ceiling of the escalator shaft. In April, Desmond Fennell issued a judgement exonerating the paint from causing the flashover. However, in June LRT, on new evidence, suggested that the burning paint (there were up to 15 coats on the escalator ceiling) had released unburnt gases that produced a fireball, which was propelled by the up-draught of the fire into the booking hall. LRT's plan for controlled burning of unburnt paint on the escalator shaft to determine its role was vetoed on safety grounds. Tests done did not show the paint to be especially flammable.

It seems to be agreed that once the flames reached the booking hall, the paint on the suspended ceiling there caught light and it took only a few seconds for the fire to spread as a sheet of flame across most of it. It was further fuelled now by a builder's wooden hoarding, painted with an incorrect mixture of paints which made it highly flammable and smoke producing, and a store of plywood behind it.

The fire was contained in the escalator and booking hall area although thick smoke filled all the passageways. The booking hall was devastated, with partly melted ticket machines and the skeleton of the booking office left standing. But there was no evidence of fire in the machinery room below the escalator, and the upper part of the escalator below the seat of the fire was amazingly untouched. Repairs were estimated at over £10 million.

Although the unusual features of this fire and their tragic consequences could not have been predicted, much could have been done to prevent the combination of circumstances which

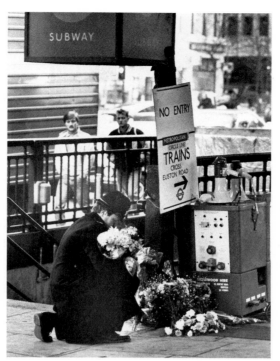

Left: a policeman placing flowers from the public outside one of the charred entrances to the station. Many of these tributes were for fireman Colin Townsley, the only fireman to die in the disaster.
Below: the funeral procession of Station Officer Townsley pauses outside King's Cross. His coffin was borne on the turntable ladder of one of his vehicles, decorated with his team's own tribute – 'GUV'.

Right: the panel appointed by the Department of Transport to head the inquiry into the fire: (left to right) Major Anthony King, Mr Desmond Fennell QC, Prof Bernard Crossland and Dr Alan Roberts.

Below: a fire inspector viewing the damage to the main ticket hall, where most of the victims died.

allowed the fire to happen at all. LRT, as the body responsible for running the Underground, came in for fierce criticism, particularly for failing to learn lessons from previous fires and implement safety recommendations. Examples relevant to this fire include fitting metal side panels and skirtings on escalators and cleaning escalators more frequently and thoroughly using modern methods. Also, no evacuation plan or procedure had been worked out, appropriate escape routes were unknown or unavailable and staff safety-training was inadequate.

A vital area found wanting during the fire was that of communications. A series of breakdowns in communication, both within the emergency services and LRT and between them, increased confusion and delays and, according to the inquiry, actually hampered the way in which the fire was tackled. Problems included inadequate or incompatible equipment, loss of contact with individuals, including with firemen underground, and essential information not passed on or seriously delayed.

LRT admitted that passenger safety had not been a high enough priority. They listed over 100 steps to be taken, costing over £30 million, to prevent a repeat of the disaster. They introduced a total ban on smoking throughout the Underground and a new programme of escalator cleaning, but there is still much room for improvement to prevent the possibility of similar disasters in future.